Tenerife

by Andrew Sanger

Andrew Sanger is a well-established travel
journalist who has contributed to a wide
range of popular magazines and most British
newspapers. He is the author of many travel
guides, including *AA Explorer Israel* and
AA Essential Lanzarote & Fuerteventura.

Above: *the view from Mirador de la Garañona,
near El Sauzel*

AA Publishing

Above: *a resident of Loro Parque, Puerto de la Cruz*

Written by Andrew Sanger
Revised (2002) by Lindsay Hunt

First published 2000. Reprinted Feb and Aug 2000, Feb and Sep 2001, Feb 2002.
Second edition 2002. Reprinted April 2003
This edition 2004

© Automobile Association Developments Limited 2002
Maps © Automobile Association Developments Limited 2002

Published by AA Publishing, a trading name of Automobile Association Developments Limited, whose registered office is Millstream, Maidenhead Road, Windsor, Berkshire SL4 5GD. Registered number 1878835.

Automobile Association Developments Limited retains the copyright in the original edition © 2000 and in all subsequent editions, reprints and amendments.

A CIP catalogue record for this book is available from the British Library.

The contents of this publication are believed correct at the time of printing. Nevertheless, AA Publishing accept no responsibility for errors, omissions or changes in the details given, or for the consequences of readers' reliance on this information. This does not affect your statutory rights. Assessments of attractions, hotels and restaurants are based upon the author's own experience and contain subjective opinions that may not reflect the publisher's opinion or a reader's experience. We have tried to ensure accuracy, but things do change, so please let us know if you have any comments or corrections.

Colour separation: Chroma Graphics (Overseas) Pte Limited, Singapore
Printed and bound in Italy by Printer Trento Srl

A01641

Find out more about AA Publishing and the wide range of travel publications and services the AA provides by visiting our web site at www.theAA.com

Contents

About this Book

KEY TO SYMBOLS

➕ map reference to the maps found in the What to See section

✉ address or location

☎ telephone number

🕐 opening times

🍴 restaurant or café on premises or nearby

Ⓜ nearest underground train station

🚌 nearest bus/tram route

🚆 nearest overground train station

🚢 ferry crossings and boat excursions

✈ travel by air

ℹ tourist information

♿ facilities for visitors with disabilities

✋ admission charge

↔ other places of interest nearby

❓ other practical information

➤ indicates the page where you will find a fuller description

This book is divided into five sections to cover the most important aspects of your visit to Tenerife.

Viewing Tenerife pages 5–14
An introduction to Tenerife by the author.
Tenerife's Features
Essence of Tenerife
The Shaping of Tenerife
Peace and Quiet
Famous of Tenerife & La Gomera

Top Ten pages 15–26
The author's choice of the Top Ten places to see in Tenerife and La Gomera, each with practical information.

What to See pages 27–90
The three main areas of Tenerife, and La Gomera, each with a brief introduction and an alphabetical listing of the main attractions.
Practical information
Snippets of 'Did you know…' information
4 suggested walks
4 suggested tours
2 features

Where To… pages 91–116
Listings of the best places to eat, stay, shop, take the children and be entertained.

4

Practical Matters pages 117–24
A highly visual section containing essential travel information.

Maps
All map references are to the individual maps found in the What to See section of this guide.

For example, Puerto de la Cruz has the reference ➕ 28C4 – indicating the page on which the map is located and the grid square in which the town is to be found. A list of the maps that have been used in this travel guide can be found in the index.

Prices
Where appropriate, an indication of the cost of an establishment is given by £ signs:
£££ denotes higher prices, ££ denotes average prices, while £ denotes lower charges.

Star Ratings
Most of the places described in this book have been given a separate rating:
✪✪✪ Do not miss
✪✪ Highly recommended
✪ Worth seeing

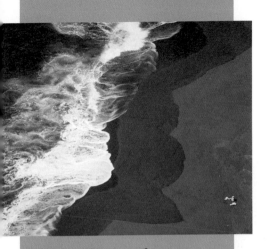

Viewing
Tenerife

Above: *looking down on the beach
from Mirador de la Garañona*
Right: *traditional dress at the Fiesta
Romera, Santa Cruz*

Andrew Sanger's Tenerife

The Canaries
There are 13 islands altogether in the volcanic Canary Islands archipelago, seven of them populated (the other six are tiny). Home to the native Guanches from about 500 BC, the Canary Islands were claimed by the Spanish in the 15th century. Though distant from the mainland, they remain administratively part of Spain.

A layer of tourism clings to the surface of Tenerife. That's not all bad – it's a prosperous tradition that dates back to the mid-19th century. Most visitors stay in sun-baked southern parts of the island where locals have rarely lived, and then usually remain there throughout their visit. But tourism, if outwardly benign, is never harmless: Europe's most popular winter sun destination has suffered from ill-judged development and unseen damage to the environment.

For me, the challenge is to get beneath that surface. Peel back the layer of tourism and you'll discover that Tenerife is not just a holiday isle, it's colonial Spain: a reminder of the *conquistadores*, an immediate sense of Spain's enterprise, power and wealth centuries ago. The Canaries feel close to the colonies in Latin America, where so many *Tinerfeños* went to live.

Yet here too is the Spain of today. Take a side turn, explore the villages, get into the hills, or the backstreets of Santa Cruz or La Laguna, and holiday land seems to vanish like morning mist. Here are the real bars and *restaurantes*, the plazas and glazed tiles and the sounds and the people of the Iberian peninsula.

However, that too can be peeled back to reveal another level. Leave the villages and backstreets behind, walk alone in the balmy, luxuriant hills, or in the desolate Cañadas. The Guanches are long gone, but there's an air of mystery about Tenerife that these native islanders bequeathed. Through them, I see that Tenerife belongs neither to the tourists nor to the Spanish, but to the Atlantic, to Africa, and to the snow-capped volcano that gave the island its Guanche name.

Above: *forest near Vilaflor, which means the 'flower town'*

Tenerife's Features

Position

Tenerife lies in the western half of the Canary Islands archipelago, just under 500km north of the Tropic of Cancer and only about 300km from the coast of Western Sahara, in Africa. La Gomera lies 32km from Tenerife's southwestern shore.

Size

The largest of the Canary Islands, Tenerife (pronounced *Ten-air-reef-eh* in Spanish) covers 2,057sq km. It's 130km across at its widest point, and 90km from north to south. By contrast, La Gomera, its next-door neighbour, is the second smallest of the Canaries, just 23km by 25km.

People

Only 700,000 people live on Tenerife, and about 20,000 on La Gomera. They're outnumbered by four million tourists annually.

Climate

Like the other Canary Islands, Tenerife and La Gomera are strongly influenced by the prevailing trade winds, bringing moist air or rain – but only to the north. The south of Tenerife and La Gomera remain almost rain-free, though there can be winter cloud. Any rain that does fall normally comes between October and February. Average daytime temperatures are about 25°C in summer and 19°C in winter. Both islands can be windy, especially on the west.

Language

Spanish is the language of the Canary Islands, with a few indigenous words still in use. English is widely spoken (especially at tourist resorts) though often not very well.

A Long Way from Spain
Though Spanish, Tenerife is much closer to the Sahara than to Spain – only around 300km from the coast of Africa, the island lies some 1,500km from Spain. Until the start of air travel in the 1950s, Tenerife was remote and little visited.

A huge bronze sculpture of a theatrical mask dominates the steps of the Teatro Guimerá in Santa Cruz

Essence of Tenerife

Tenerife is like two places in one. In the north it's Spanish and lived-in, with working towns and villages. In the south it's a basking holiday land of vibrant entertainment, resorts and hotels, devoted to giving millions of visitors a fortnight of fun. While the north has an almost tropical, productive lushness, the south is rainless and dry.

The combination of the two gives Tenerife tremendous appeal. For many visitors nothing can tear them away from days in the sun and nights on the town. For others it's a delight to explore the 'real' Tenerife, getting to know this beautiful volcanic land and its people. And some, of course, enjoy both sides of Tenerife.

Above: the founder of the Museo Municipal de Bellas Artes, Santa Cruz

Below: children enjoy a local fiesta

THE **10** ESSENTIALS

If you only have a short time to visit Tenerife, or would like to get a really complete picture of the island, here are the essentials:

• **Go up Pico del Teide**
The high point of Tenerife, a snow-capped dormant volcano worshipped by the Guanches, the original inhabitants of the island. From here you can see almost the whole of the Canary Islands (▶ 18).

• **Experience Playa de las Américas** Leave the real world behind and enter the package holiday dreamland, in a purpose-built town of artificial beaches, all-night discos, English pubs and restaurants that proudly

boast 'No Spanish Food Served Here!' (▶ 74–5).

• **Go bananas** Eat Tenerife bananas, have them flambéed for dessert, drink banana liqueur, buy souvenirs made of banana leaves and visit Bananera El Guanche (▶ 55) – all because bananas are an important crop here.

• **Eat a Canarian stew** Try *potaje, rancho canario* or *puchero* – vegetables and meat simmered to a savoury perfection. With bread, locals consider it a complete meal.

• **Get spicy** You must try the pleasantly spicy local sauce called *mojo*. Served

with fish or *papas arrugadas* (wrinkly potatoes), it's the most Canarian thing on the menu.

• **Drink a local wine**
One of the first big successes for colonial Tenerife was the development of drinkable wines to rival those in mainland Spain. The island's wines have remained important ever since. La Gomera, too, has good local wines.

• **Get out of the resorts**
Walk, drive or cycle, but one way or another see the Tenerife most tourists miss.

• **Watch a whale** Join one of the boat excursions to see the whales and dolphins which live just off southern Tenerife and La Gomera (▶ 111).

• **Have fun at a fiesta** It's an unusual fortnight in the Tenerife calendar that doesn't have at least one fiesta. Ask the tourist office what's on next.

• **Go to another island**
Take the ferry to La Gomera for a truly unspoiled Canary island. If you're on La Gomera, take the boat trip over just to visit Pico del Teide.

Above: *a wine cellar sign in Icod de los Vinos, a town justly famed for its wines*

Above: *sand was brought from the Sahara to create Playa de las Teresitas*

Inset: *nightlife at Playa de las Américas*

The Shaping of Tenerife

2–20 million years ago
Volcanic eruptions create the Canary Islands, starting with the most easterly and moving west. Tenerife appears 10 million years ago.

c500 BC
Tenerife is peopled by the Guanches (Old Canarian meaning 'son of Tenerife'), believed to have been Berbers, nomadic pastoralists of North Africa. When the first Europeans arrive much later, the tribes of the islands still mummify their leaders and speak a language recognisably derived from the Berbers.

12th–1st century BC
Phoenician and other sailors visit the Canary Islands. From antiquity the archipelago is known as The Fortunate Isles.

c25 BC
On behalf of the Romans, Juba II of Mauritania sends an expedition to explore the Fortunate Isles. One island is named Canaria for its wild dogs (Latin *canis*, dog); the islands take the name Canaries.

2nd century AD
The Greek geographer Ptolemy puts the Canary Islands on the map, placing the prime meridian through El Hierro, the edge of the known world.

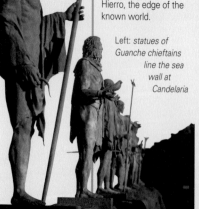

Left: *statues of Guanche chieftains line the sea wall at Candelaria*

1312
Genoese sailor Lancelotto Malocello visits Fuerteventura and Lanzarote (which is a corruption of his name), the first European colonist in the Canaries.

1350–1450
Assorted raiders and slavers pause at the Canaries for the purpose of capturing slaves.

1402
Two Norman adventurers, Gadifer de la Salle and Jean de Béthencourt, set out to conquer the Canaries. Although only taking Lanzarote, they claim all the islands for the king of Spain, who financed their trip.

Early 1400s
On more easterly islands, Norman and Spanish settlers enslave the Guanche natives and establish European-style farming villages, but Tenerife remains unconquered.

1493–95
A determined and ruthless Spanish colonist, Alonso Fernández de Lugo, financed by Genoese merchants and equipped with 1,000 mercenaries, attacks Tenerife. Most of his men are ambushed and killed by the Guanches a year later. In November

1494 de Lugo returns with more men and conquers the island, killing thousands of Guanches. Land handed out to investors in his expedition are developed as sugar plantations. Portuguese and Spanish labourers are shipped in to work the new farms.

16th–17th centuries
Destructive French, English, Dutch and Arab pirates and privateers harass Tenerife, attracted by the merchant ships coming from the New World and pausing at Santa Cruz. Tenerife's various fortifications date from this period.

18th century
Grapes are planted and soon wine is an important product. Tenerife becomes a civilised and cultured hideaway for European nobility and wealthy traders.

1797
Rear Admiral Nelson attacks Santa Cruz in order to take the town, seize treasure offloaded by the Spanish ship *Principe de Asturias*, and to show the French who is supreme on the high seas. In the only failure of his career, Nelson retreats having lost his right arm after being injured by grapeshot.

19th century
The wine trade collapses, but is replaced first by the cultivation of cochineal beetles (for their dye), which are raised on plantations of cacti, and then by bananas, soon the main crop. The banana boats also carry passengers, and the island becomes a fashionable resort for wealthy British scholars, writers and artists. One of the first guidebooks is written – *Tenerife and its Six Satellites* (by Olivia Stone, 1887).

1914–18
The Great War causes massive emigration.

1936
Francisco Franco, military governor or Capitán-General of the Canary Islands, based on Tenerife, plans a right-wing coup to take over Spain. On 18 July, the Spanish Civil War (1936–39) starts with the nationalist takeover of Tenerife. A week later Franco has control of all the Canary Islands. He leaves Tenerife for Morocco to plan an attack on the Spanish mainland.

Early 1960s
Package holdays to the Canaries begins. Tenerife is immediately successful, with the transformation of Puerto de la Cruz into a modern resort.

1978
International airport Reina Sofía opens on the south coast. Playa de las Américas begins to be developed.

Late 1980s
Almost all Canary bananas now go to Spain.

1980–90s
Tourism reaches huge proportions and becomes the island's main source of income.

2000
Plans are made to take tourism up-market and reduce visitor numbers.

Below: the international airport at Reina Sofía

Peace & Quiet

Despite Tenerife's clamour and crowds, much of the island remains tranquil – it is easy to escape from the excesses of tourism. Remember too that most tourists wake up late: even popular spots enjoy relative peace in the mornings.

The desert-like south possesses a magical quality of stillness and silence. In the central uplands, pine-covered

slopes reach into a rocky terrain carved by the volcanic power of Pico del Teide. The lush green northern hills, draped with perennial wild blossom, are a delight that few visitors discover. Almost anywhere off the beaten track, the country is coloured with masses of nasturtiums and hibiscus, marigolds and carnations, geraniums and hanging bougainvillea.

Quiet country paths are a feature of the island and make a pleasant break for an interesting stroll, getting to know Tenerife's character and landscapes. Keen ramblers could spend a fortnight on the island and barely see another foreigner, taking the more isolated trails

Clearly marked paths lead walkers through the stunning mountain countryside around Chinamada

to climb and explore the interior.

You don't need to be a strong walker to discover all this. Car drivers will soon find picnic spots away from the main roads. ICONA, the Spanish conservation agency, has created beautifully located picnic places all over the island. Some 1,700 species of plant life flourish here, and much of

Wild flowers in the Parque Nacional del Teide

12

the fauna and flora is unique to the island. It's worth adding that Tenerife is mercifully free of troublesome insects and there are no poisonous snakes.

On the dry southern shores cacti and palms thrive, while along the northern and western coasts semi-tropical varieties abound. Here are woods of mimosa, jacaranda and rubber trees, wild roses and poinsettia, and, of course, that Tenerife marvel, the mighty dragon tree (*Dracaena draco*) and the gentle bird-of-paradise flower (*Strelitzia*).

In and around the Parque Nacional del Teide, the greenery of the Valle de la Orotava contrasts with the drama of Las Cañadas and the intriguing rare plants of Pico del Teide. The most striking is the giant bugloss (*Echium wildpretii*) with amazing erect red flower clusters as much as two metres long – a true native found only on the Canary Islands. High on the slopes, the Teide violet (*Viola cheiranthifolia*) lives only here. The Teide daisy and Teide broom, too, are endemic. The mountainsides are covered with pine and palm. On upper slopes pockets survive of the once extensive *Laurisilva*, or forests of Canary laurel (*Larus canariensis*).

Take a boat across to La Gomera for a more perfect peace. Get well away from San Sebastián, where the ferry disembarks, heading west into the hinterland of this undeveloped Canary Island, deeply scored with *barrancos* (gorges). Its central mountain region is thickly covered with Canary laurel forest, and on the coasts it is still possible to find sun, sea – and solitude.

Trees in the Valle de la Orotava rising above a layer of cloud

Spectacular flowering cacti thrive on Tenerife

Famous of Tenerife & La Gomera

The Franco Connection
General Francisco Franco, the dictator who ruled Spain with an iron hand from 1939 to 1975, launched his coup from Tenerife, where he lived as Capitán-General for four months in 1936. For old times' sake he took a holiday on the island in 1953.

Nelson's mission was to capture Spanish treasure ships rumoured to be in the Canary Islands

Tomás de Iriarte

The small population of the island of Tenerife, largely illiterate until the 1970s, has produced few famous sons. One of the most important was 18th-century satirical writer and translator Tomás de Iriarte (1750–91), whose works were highly successful on the mainland (► 56). They included a collection of fables, *Fábulas Literarias*, and many translations of the Roman poet and satirist Horace.

Beatriz de Bobadilla

A great beauty at the Spanish court, Beatriz (c1455–1508) was a mistress of Ferdinand V, whose queen, Isabella of Castile, contrived to remove her to La Gomera. She married its governor, Count Hernán Peraza, who was murdered by the Guanches for his cruelty (► 87). Beatriz took revenge on the native Gomerans and had hundreds put to death or sold into slavery. She continued to rule La Gomera in her own right. In 1498 she married Alonso Fernández de Lugo, conqueror of Tenerife. She was eventually summoned back to court in Madrid, where she was poisoned (almost certainly on the orders of Queen Isabella).

Horatio Nelson

Horatio Nelson (1758–1805), like some modern tourists, didn't so much visit Tenerife as invade it. Then rear admiral, his attack on Santa Cruz in 1797 was the only failure of his illustrious career in the service of the British Crown. He was sent to seize treasure offloaded by a Spanish ship, but his forces were insufficient for the task; Nelson lost his right arm in the process. He and his men were generously treated by doctors on the island.

Christopher Columbus

By far the most famous person associated with the island of La Gomera is Christopher Columbus (1451–1506), the explorer and entrepreneur who stayed there before setting out to discover whether a westward trade route existed to the Indies. His first visit in 1492 was in order to take on supplies before the pioneering Atlantic crossing. Becoming friendly with the island's countess Beatriz de Bobadilla, he visited La Gomera twice more during his Atlantic voyages.

Top Ten

Above: *Garachico, from San Juan del Repard*
Right: *the restored façade of the Casa de los Balcones, La Orotava*

15

1
Casa de los Balcones, La Orotava

28C4

Calle San Francisco 3, La Orotava

922 330629

Mon–Fri 8:30–6:30, Sat 8:30–5, Sun 8:30–1

Restaurants and bars in Plaza de la Constitución

345 and 350 (Puerto de la Cruz–La Orotava) every 20–30 min.; 348 same route once daily

None

Museum cheap; courtyard and craft shop free

La Orotava (▶ 65)

The Casa is famous for the intricately carved balconies in its courtyard

The most famous sight in the sedate Spanish colonial hilltown of La Orotava is an intriguing 17th-century mansion

Pretty potted geraniums decorate the balconies looking over Calle San Francisco. It's not the balconies on the outside, though, that give the house its name: enter the impressive front doors and you will find the exquisitely carved wooden balconies of the courtyard. Here abundant refreshing greenery, earthenware pots and an old wine press give a cool, elegant air. The building's history is told in the museum upstairs: originally it consisted of two separate houses built in 1632 as homes for prosperous colonists.

Downstairs in the busy souvenir and craft shop, a major stop-off point for coach tours, an additional attraction is local craftspeople demonstrating how to roll a cigar, weave a basket, or paint sand in readiness for the big Corpus Christi celebrations. This unusual shop sells, in addition to popular souvenirs, a wide range of high-quality items such as Spanish and Canarian lace and linen, and traditional handcrafted Canarian embroideries. Some small items – such as handkerchiefs – give an opportunity to buy good quality local goods at affordable prices.

Some of the embroideries are made on the premises, as the Casa de los Balcones also serves as a highly regarded school for embroidery. For over 50 years the school has been training small numbers of pupils in the traditional methods and designs of Canarian embroidery, which would perhaps have disappeared altogether if not for its efforts.

2
Drago Milenario

The drago *or dragon tree is a species peculiar to the Canary Islands, and this amazing, ancient example has become an island emblem.*

Icod de los Vinos is home to the legendary dragon tree

Just how old is this extraordinary tree? The age of the 'Thousand-Year-Old Dragon Tree' is often exaggerated to two or even three thousand years – in reality, this majestic specimen, the oldest known, probably dates back about 600 years.

More remarkable perhaps is that the species itself – *Dracaena draco*, closely related to the yucca – has barely evolved since the age of the dinosaurs. It has long been an object of fascination, not just among modern botanists and naturalists, but among all who are sensitive to magic and mystery. That's partly because of its curious form, growing like a bundle of separate trunks clinging together before bursting to create the *drago*'s distinctive mushroom shape. Weirdest of all is the *drago*'s strange resin, which turns as red as blood on contact with the air. Though nothing is known of Guanche beliefs, many people insist that the *drago* was worshipped by these first inhabitants of the island, who did use its resin for embalming.

Standing 17m high and with a diameter of 6m, the Drago Milenario is the main attraction at Icod de los Vinos, an attractive little wine town on the west coast. One of Tenerife's largest Guanche settlements stood here when the Europeans arrived, and the Drago Milenario was already mature when the Spanish took control. The gigantic tree is now protected in a garden, while bars and souvenir shops around cash in on the tree's mystique. Different from the rest, and an attraction in itself, is the traditional and pretty shop, Casa del Drago.

28B4

Parque del Drago (by the church), Plaza de la Constitucion 1, Icod de los Vinos

922 330629

Moderate (free view from church square)

Bars and cafés nearby (£)

354 and 363 (Puerto de la Cruz–Icod) every 30 min.

Icod de los Vinos (► 64), Garachico (► 20)

Icod holds a Dragon Tree Festival in Sep

3
Pico del Teide

28C3

Parque Nacional del Teide

Nearest eating places are the *parador* and at El Portillo

348 runs from Puerto de la Cruz to the Teide cable car once daily, leaving Puerto at 9:15 and reaching the cable car at 11:15. The return trip is at 4:15. Bus 342 runs from Playa de las Américas to Teide cable car once daily, leaving Playa at 9:15 and arriving at the cable car at 11:15. The return trip is at 3:40. Note, the bus times can be unreliable

None

Cable car expensive; free on foot

Cable car hotline ☎ 922 383711, AM only ⏰ Last descent 5PM; doesn't run in windy weather

The highest mountain in all Spain is an active – but sleeping – volcano, soaring majestically above the Atlantic island it helped to create.

Pico del Teide was aflame as Christopher Columbus passed this way. The sailors took it for an ill omen, Columbus for a good one. Before the Spanish conquest, the Guanche people of Tenerife – and the other islands too – revered this conical mountain crested with snow and fire. It could erupt again at any time, though for a century or so at a stretch the volcano remains dormant, its occasional murmurings no more threatening than the purring of a sleeping lion. The most recent eruption was a small one in 1898, and the volcano has been quiet since; it has made some noises of late and scientists are monitoring any risk.

Over many millennia, Pico del Teide's eruptions have added more and more land to the island of Tenerife, though the terrain all around the volcano is a blasted landscape of twisted rock and debris, a devastation that thrills and amazes visitors. This region now has protected status within the Parque Nacional del Teide (➤ 66). Although not an attraction, not an entertainment, not even particularly accessible, and offering nothing but its dignified presence, Pico del Teide ranks first among the 'musts' of Tenerife.

Pico del Teide is a mere remnant of the original Tenerife volcano, the cone of which at some point blew itself to pieces in a massive eruption. The relics of the cone surround Pico del Teide in a ring of lesser volcanic outlets, which are known as the Caldera de las Cañadas.

The 3,718m mountain does not always permit people to visit, guarding itself in mist, snow or powerful winds – sometimes even when the weather is fine down on the coast. In the height of summer, heat can be a problem, often reaching 40°C. However, on fine, calm days the summit can be approached either on foot in around 3 hours or, more usual, by *teleférico* (cable car) in 8 minutes. The cable car can, however, involve long waits (over an hour is not unusual).

Permits are required for the final 163m above the terminal, a steep scramble on loose scree (see right).

A single well-worn footpath makes its way to the summit from the car park below Montaña Blanca, close to the lower cable-car terminal. Only experienced walkers, properly equipped, should attempt any other route. It is easier to walk up than down, so consider taking the cable car one way. The path first climbs Montaña Blanca, which you may consider rewarding enough by itself. Bear in mind that altitude sickness may be a problem, so go slowly to minimise this risk.

On this final climb to the top, there's a whiff of sulphur in the air and a real sense that Pico del Teide means business. You pass impressive smoke holes some 50m across. Take this climb gently, carry water with you, wear a sunhat and sunglasses, and carry a light sweater to wear at the summit. Whether by foot or by *teleférico*, the view is dramatic and the experience unforgettable.

Above: *Pico del Teide with Los Roques de Garcia in the foreground*
Left: *approaching the summit of Pico del Teide*

Permits to climb the last 163m to the peak from the cable-car station are restricted to 150 per day. They are availble from the National Park office ⊠ Calle Emilio Calzadilla 5, near Plaza del Principe, Santa Cruz ⏱ Mon–Fri 9–2 ☎ 922 290129. All applicants require passports. Check the cable car and weather before starting.

19

4
Garachico

✝ 28B4

ℹ Calle Estéban de Ponte 5
☎ 922 133461

♿ None

🍽 Isla Baja (££) for fish, and
Casa Ramón (£) for
Canarian dishes

🚌 363 (Puerto de la
Cruz–Buenavista) hourly

♿ None

↔ Icod de los Vinos (► 64),
Drago Milenario (► 17)

❓ Romería de San Roque,
Aug (► 116); Feria
Artesanía (craft fair)
monthly, first Sun

❓ For the best view of the
lava flow that engulfed
Garachico, take the
mountain road (TF1421)
up to Mirador de
Garachico

For 200 years, vessels set sail laden with wine and sugar from Garachico, Tenerife's busiest port. Then in one night the harbour was destroyed.

Above: *the fortress of San Miguel stands guard above the sea*

Created as a port by Genoese entrepreneur Cristobal de Ponte in 1496, the original Garachico became a prosperous colonial town and so it remained for two centuries. Today it lies partly buried beneath the present town – on 5 May 1706 the Volcan Negro (just south of the town) roared into life, pouring lava through Garachico and into its harbour.

The islanders laid out new streets on the land formed by the lava. But the harbour – originally much larger – was never to recover, and Garachico, with its fine mansions and cobbled streets, became a handsome relic.

Around the main square, Glorieta de San Francisco, the old Franciscan monastery, **Convento de San Francisco**, pre-dates the eruption. It now houses the Casa de la Cultura, which hosts events and exhibitions (go inside just to see the pretty interiors and two courtyards), and the Museo de las Ciencias Naturales, a modest mix of local flora, fauna and history. Don't miss the pictures showing the route of the lava flow.

Parque Puerta de Tierra, a lush sunken garden alongside Plaza de Juan González de la Torre, was part of Garachico's harbour. A huge arch that marked the port entrance has been dug out of the lava and re-erected in the square, while close by an enormous wine press also pre-dates the eruption.

For a tremendous view, go up to the roof of **Castillo de San Miguel**. This dark 16th-century fortress of the counts of Gomera, emblazoned with their crests, stood firm as the lava flowed past. Today it contains a little museum and craft stall. Steps lead down to the sea, where the lava has made pleasing rocky pools.

Convento de San Francisco

✉ Glorieta de San Francisco

🕐 Mon–Fri 9–7, Sat 9–6,
Sun, hols 9–2

♿ None

👆 Moderate

Castillo de San Miguel

☎ 922 830000

🕐 Daily 10–6

♿ None

👆 Cheap

5

Loro Parque,
Puerto de la Cruz

The premier family attraction on Tenerife is a tropical wildlife park that mixes conservation, education, entertainment and fun.

This is one of the original tourist attractions on Tenerife, located in the island's first holiday resort. From simple beginnings in 1972 as a parrot park (which is what Loro Parque means), it is now an internationally acclaimed award-winning wildlife theme park, an extravaganza of tropical gardens, a dolphinarium and sea-life centre, with related attractions and rides. Covering 12.5ha, with over 2,000 palm trees, it's home to a colony of gorillas, and has a water zone where the ever-popular sea lions and dolphins seem to relish their role as a holiday entertainment. The park's aquarium tunnel, believed to be the longest in the world, is a transparent underwater walkway 18.5m long. As you walk along, sharks slip through the water, just a few centimetres away. There are flamingos, crocodiles, cranes, giant turtles, jaguars, monkeys and a Nocturnal Bat Cave. A recent addition is Planet Penguin. A special effects cinema, Natura Vision, takes you on a trip through other wildlife centres around the world.

Parrots, however, remain an important element of the park. There are over 300 species living here – the world's largest collection. The birds are being studied, and the Park is engaged in important breeding and conservation work. While endangered parrot species may be confined, the more common varieties are used in parrot shows several times each day. These feature clever tricks and elaborate entertainments that the parrots have learned to perform.

28C4

1.5km west of Plaza del Charco near Punta Brava

922 373841

Daily 8:30–6:30 (last admission 5PM)

Good

Expensive

Choice on site, including a pizzeria (££) and a self-service buffet (£)

Free shuttle bus from Avenida de Colón (near Lido) and Plaza del Charco every 20 min.

Puerto de la Cruz (▶ 54)

The attractions of Loro Parque extend to many more species than just parrots

6
Los Gigantes

✚ 28A3

✉ 2km from Puerto de Santiago on the west coast

ℹ Edificio Seguro del Sol 36–37, Playa de la Arena ☎ 922 860348

♿ None

🍴 Bars and restaurants near the marina (£–££)

🚌 325 (Puerto de la Cruz) or 473 to the south coast resorts

🚢 Excursions from Puerto de Santiago, Playa de las Américas and Los Cristianos

↔ Garachico (➤ 20), Pico del Teide (➤ 18)

The black sand beach at Los Gigantes

These stupendous sheer cliffs are called The Giants, an apt description of a rock face that soars 600m from blue sea to blue sky.

One of Tenerife's most breathtaking sights is best seen from a boat: properly known as Acantilados de los Gigantes, the soaring dark rock face rising 600m from the Atlantic marks the abrupt edge of northwestern Tenerife's Teno Massif. There's nothing more to the site but its sheer grandeur, but that's enough to attract almost all visitors to Tenerife. Come by car or coach and join a sightseeing boat when you arrive, or, perhaps better, take a boat excursion from one of the resorts. Either way, it's not until you see another boat cruising gently at the foot of these cliffs that their true majesty becomes clear.

The cliffs rise from one end of a pleasant bay called La Canalita. At the other end of the bay there's a small resort with a quiet, civilised feel and a black sand beach called Playa de los Guios. Being slightly remote, it preserves a calm holiday atmosphere now rare on the island. The cliffs and the sea guarantee that this little resort cannot expand much.

South of Los Gigantes, however, the coast has been heavily developed, mostly with apartment blocks. An excellent black sand beach called Playa de la Arena near the former fishing village of Puerto de Santiago creates a focal point to the urban sprawl.

7

Mercado Nuestra Señora de África, Santa Cruz

Tenerife's main produce market, the Market of Our Lady of Africa, is a dazzle of colour and energy, a picture of the island's abundance.

 35C2

 Just off Calle de San Sebastián, at the south end of Puente Servador, Santa Cruz ☎ 922 606090

The generosity of the Canaries and their surrounding ocean, and their ready access to all the abundance of the rest of Spain, are daily apparent in the wonderful displays in this lively and atmospheric enclosed market. Flowers fill the eye, alongside the colours of myriad fruits and vegetables, and other stalls are laden with fish and meat. You'll find small live animals, a multitude of curious peasant cheeses made of cow's, sheep's or goat's milk (or sometimes all three) and home-made honey. Here too traders sell cheap cassettes and CDs – often of foot-stamping Spanish and Latin American music. Interestingly, all is neat and orderly, with a surprising tidiness and efficiency.

The market is located near the heart of the old quarter of Tenerife's capital town, not far from the lanes of a red-light district, and usually spills out into these surrounding streets, where stalls sell 'dry goods' – kitchenware, fabrics and household items. The market entrance itself is a circular arch, leading straight into the flower stalls. Beyond lies a veritable bazaar within the central courtyard.

There's officially no market here on Sunday, but that's when the big weekly *rastro* sets up outside the market hall. A *rastro* is a mixed flea market and craft market, where an array of stallholders from home and abroad sell a hotch-potch of cheap souvenirs, second-rate factory-made 'craft' items, leather goods, assorted cast-offs and secondhand items, as well as plenty of genuine high-quality arts and crafts. Philatelists will love it: stamps are a particular speciality of several stallholders.

 Mon–Sat 8–1 (Sun *rastro* market 10–2)

Few

Santa Cruz (► 32)

 Watch out for pickpockets! Tourists at the market are seen as easy prey

Above: *visitors to the market are greeted by an array of flowers*

23

8
Museo de Antropología de Tenerife

The traditional exterior of the Casa de Carta

A fascinating collection of Canary Islands folk culture, housed in a fine restored country mansion, one of the most beautiful buildings on the island.

✚ 29D5

✉ Carretera Tacoronte–Valle de Guerra, 25km from Puerto de la Cruz

☎ 922 150534

🕐 Tue–Sun 10–8

♿ Few

✋ Moderate (Sun free)

🍴 In and around nearby Tacoronte (££)

🚌 Call Tacoronte Bus Information ☎ 922 561807

↔ El Sauzal (➤ 44)

This beautiful, low, white-painted Canarian farmhouse and country mansion dates back to the end of the 17th century, and is one of Tenerife's prettiest architectural gems. The building is an exquisite arrangement of carved wooden doors, balconies, porticos and patios. It stands among tropical gardens in the countryside overlooking the village of Valle de Guerra.

For centuries the home of the Carta family of regional administrators, the building now houses the Tenerife Anthropology Museum. Reconstructed rooms reveal much about rural life in Tenerife, and there are examples of all the island's folk arts and crafts. Inside, 14 exhibition rooms with their galleries are used to re-create appealing little glimpses of ordinary life in the rural Tenerife of past times. The principal displays are of weaving, needlework and pottery, as well as farm tools, fabrics, clothing, ceramics and furniture.

The most interesting exhibits are of traditional Canarian dress from the 18th century onwards, highlighting the small but important differences of style and colour between one island and the next. Embroidered and patterned festival clothes, wedding clothes and everyday workwear are on show. The weaving and sewing rooms show how these clothes would have been made in the past.

9
Nuestra Señora de la Concepción, La Laguna

When Guanche leaders were 'persuaded' to become Christian and submit to Spanish rule, they were brought to this grandiose church to be baptised.

The oldest church on the island, with much outstanding craftsmanship, Our Lady of the Immaculate Conception represents a landmark in Canarian history and has the status of a Spanish national shrine. Its greatest claim to fame is that the big glazed 16th-century baptismal font, brought here from Seville in southern Spain, was used to 'convert' defeated Guanche warriors to Christianity. You'll find it in the *baptisterio* (baptistery) set to one side of the main entrance, with family trees displayed above.

Though much changed since its foundation in 1502, even in those days the church was extraordinarily grand for a far-flung colony, with elaborately carved gilded wooden ceiling panels in Moorish design. Over the centuries, the church benefited from the finest workmanship on the island, its Gothic origins becoming overlaid with Renaissance style and then baroque decoration.

The triple-nave church has probably the grandest and richest interior on Tenerife, and rivals any other building in the Canaries. The gold and silver paintwork and metalwork are breathtaking, together with rich retables from the 17th century and later. Immediately obvious on entering the building, the extravagant woodcarving of the 18th-century pulpit is considered one of Spain's best examples of this type of work. The choir stalls, too, are beautifully carved.

The eye-catching seven-storey tower, dating from the 17th century, has a distinctive Moorish look and is the principal landmark of this historic town.

The side altar captures the eye with its gilded tiers

29E5

Plaza del la Concepción, La Laguna

Usually Mon–Fri 11–1, 5–8. Sat–Sun services only

Few

Cheap

Tapas bars and restaurants nearby

102 (Puerto de la Cruz or Santa Cruz–La Laguna) every 30 min.

La Laguna (▶ 45)

10

Parque Nacional de Garajonay, La Gomera

A vast area of protected forest covers the central upland of La Gomera: a strange, dark wilderness of lichens, ravines and laurel canyons.

While sun beats down on the southern shore, a cooler, damper climate prevails around Mount Garajonay. Heather, ferns and lichens flourish, creating a thick carpet across the boulders and rocky slopes where the last of the native Canarian laurel woodland survives. Waterfalls and streams splash through the greenery. Walking in this wet, magical terrain among the slender, sinuous limbs of the Canary laurel (*Larus canariensis*), it is certainly hard to believe that you are in the Canary Islands. Not just laurel but also the luxuriant Canary date palm (*Phoenix canariensis*) grows here in great numbers, and there are around 400 species of native flowers, some found only at this place. There are also many rare insects and birds.

A useful starting point if you are passing is the **Centro de Visitantes** (**Visitor Centre**) at Juego de Bolas, on the north side of the forest. This gives an overview of the Park and its flora and fauna, and details all the waymarked forest walks. The centre has much else about La Gomera, including gardens, a small museum, and displays about island life over the centuries. Craftspeople demonstrate traditional skills such as weaving, pottery, basketwork and carpentry.

Easy, popular walks start at La Laguna Grande in the middle of the forest, where there's a small information centre, a woodland play area, a board showing marked trails, and a track up to a lofty *mirador* (viewpoint).

Sidebar

✚ 82B2

♿ None

✋ Free

🍴 Restaurants at La Laguna (££)

↔ Agulo (► 84), Chipude (► 84), Hermigua (► 85)

Centro de Visitantes

✉ Juego de Bolas, near Las Rosas (35km from San Sebastián)

☎ 922 800993

🕐 Tue–Sun 9:30–4:30. The craft workshops are open Tue–Fri only

♿ Few

✋ Free

Sunlight reaches through the trees to the flowers covering the forest floor

What to See

Above: *on the beach at Playa de las Teresitas*
Right: *a bronze statue near the Palacio Insular in Plaza de España, Santa Cruz*

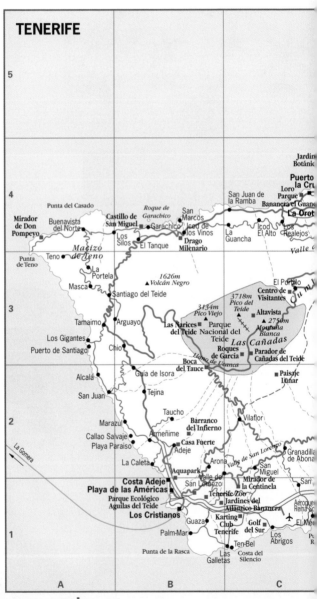

TENERIFE

5

4

Jardín Botánic

Puerto Loro **de la Cru**
Parque
Bananera el Guanc
La Orot

San Juan de
la Ramba

Roque de
Garachico San
Marcos

Punta del Casado **Castillo de**
San Miguel Garachico Icod de
Buenavista Los los Vinos
Mirador del Norte Silos La Icod Los
de Don El Tanque **Drago** Guancha El Alto Realejos
Pompeyo
Teno *Macizo* **Milenario** *Valle*

Punta La *de Teno*
de Teno Portela El Portillo

Masca *1626m* **Centro de**
▲ *Volcán Negro* **Visitantes** *Cum*

Santiago del Teide *3134m* **Altavista**
Pico Viejo *3718m*
Pico del ▲ *2750m*
Tamaimo Arguayo *Teide* *Montaña*
Las Narices *Blanca*
Los Gigantes **del Teide** Parque *Las Cañadas*
Chio Nacional del
Puerto de Santiago **Teide**
Roques **Parador de**
de García **Cañadas del Teide**
Boca
3 **del Tauce** *Llano de Ucanca*

Alcalá **Paisaje**
Guía de Isora **Lunar**
San Juan

Tejina

Taucho
Marazul Vilaflor
Barranco
Callao Salvaje Armeñime **del Infierno**
Playa Paraíso
Casa Fuerte
2 La Caleta Adeje
Granadilla
Aquapark Arona *Valle de San Lorenzo* de Abona
Costa Adeje *Valle de* San
Playa de las Américas *San Lorenzo* Miguel
Parque Ecológico **Mirador de** San
Águilas del Teide **Tenerife Zoo** **la Centinela**
Los Cristianos **Jardines del**
Guaza **Atlántico Bananera** Aéropue
Karting Reina Sc
Golf
1 Palm-Mar **Club** **del Sur** Los El Mé
Tenerife Abrigos
Ten-Bel
Punta de la Rasca **Costa del**
Las **Silencio**
Galletas

La Gomera →

A B C

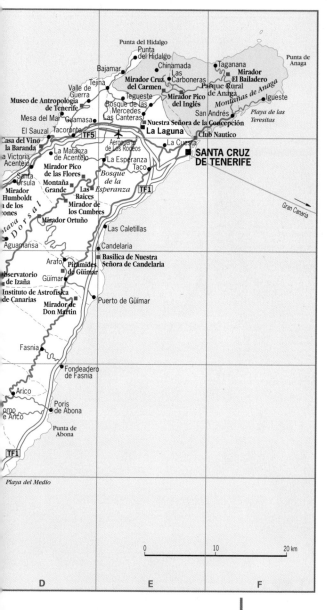

Punta del Hidalgo
Punta
del Hidalgo
Bajamar
Chinamada
Las
Carboneras
Taganana
Mirador
El Bailadero
Punta de
Anaga
Valle de
Guerra
Tejina
Mirador Cruz
del Carmen
Parque Rural
de Anaga
Montañas de Anaga
Museo de Antropología
de Tenerife
Teguesta
Mirador Pico
del Inglés
Igueste
Bosque de las
Mercedes
Las Canteras
San Andrés
Playa de las
Teresitas
Mesa del Mar
Guamasa
Nuestra Señora de la Concepción
El Sauzal
Tacoronte
La Laguna
Casa del Vino
la Baranda
a Victoria
Acentejo
TF5
Club Nautico
Aeropuerto
de Los Rodeos
La Cuesta
SANTA CRUZ
DE TENERIFE
La Matanza
de Acentejo
Santa
Úrsula
Mirador Pico
de las Flores
La Esperanza
Taco
Mirador
Humboldt
a de los
ones
Montaña
Grande
Las
Raíces
Bosque
de la
Esperanza
TF1
Octava Dorsal
Mirador de
los Cumbres
Gran Canaria
Mirador Ortuño
Las Caletillas
Aguamansa
Candelaria
Arafo
Pirámides
de Güímar
Basílica de Nuestra
Señora de Candelaria
Observatorio
de Izaña
Güímar
Instituto de Astrofísica
de Canarias
Mirador de
Don Martín
Puerto de Güímar
Fasnia
Fondeadero
de Fasnia
Arico
omo
e Arico
Poris
de Abona
Punta de
Abona
TF1
Playa del Medio

0   10   20 km

D   E   F

The North

The real life of Tenerife is all in the north. Here the whole history of Tenerife can be told, for the Guanches mainly occupied the northern half, and the Spanish too settled and cultivated this area. Until package holiday holidays took off in the 1960s, even holidaymakers rarely ventured south of Puerto de la Cruz, except for the essential excursion to Pico del Teide. As a result, almost all of the island's art, culture, its Spanish colonial legacy, and its best sightseeing, are in the north.

The climate is responsible for this: the north and northwest, facing the trade winds, catch all of Tenerife's gentle rain. Parts of this fertile half of the island are exotically verdant, with tropical flowers and greenery. That's what attracted the first aristocratic tourists, who adored the permanent springtime, rich crops and garden landscape of northern Tenerife.

> *'They make wine better than any in Spaine, they have grapes of such bignesse that they may bee compared to damsons ... for sugar, suckets, raisins of the Sunne, and many other fruits, abundance.'*
>
> RICHARD HAKLUYT,
> *Principal Navigations* (1598–1600)

---•---

The glowing altarpiece in the Iglesia de Nuestra Señora de la Concepción, Santa Cruz

Santa Cruz de Tenerife

Santa Cruz, the island's capital, still has the authentic feel and look of colonial Spain. It's not a holiday resort, but a vibrant Latin city where many Tinerfeños live and work. The name means Holy Cross of Tenerife, and comes from the crucifix planted boldly at this spot by the ruthless Spanish conqueror Alonso Fernández de Lugo, when he strode ashore in 1493 with 1,000 men to take possession of the Guanches' island home.

Below: *crowds throng one of the principal shopping streets in the centre of Santa Cruz*

🕂 29E4

ℹ️ Palacio Insular (ground floor), Plaza de España

☎ 922 239592

🕐 Mon–Fri 8–6, Sat 9–1

During the five centuries since the conquest, Santa Cruz has remained the focal point of Tenerife's culture and history. While the gaudy, multicultural Tenerife of modern tourism stays way down south, the resolutely Spanish capital has remained almost unaffected by the millions of package-holiday visitors.

Only tourists determined to know and understand the island, and looking for something more than a suntan, choose to stay here. It's also due to the diverse economy of the capital, with its oil processing, waterfront industry and deep-water harbour. Now though, Santa Cruz has polished up some of its treasures and even provides a jaunty little 'train' to take people on a tour of the sights. At the same time, holidaymakers have realised there's more to Tenerife than bierkellers and crowded black beaches, and that much of the best sightseeing is in and around Santa Cruz. The redeveloped waterfront area with its diverse shipping continues to be a source of interest, while just north of the city lies a little-know treasure, the best beach on Tenerife.

Right: *the whitewashed façade of the Iglesia de San Francisco*

What to see in Santa Cruz

IGLESIA DE NUESTRA SEÑORA DE LA CONCEPCIÓN (CHURCH OF OUR LADY OF THE CONCEPTION) ✪✪

One of the city's most important landmarks, this church is also one of its most significant historical monuments. Its attractive square tower rises from a plaza enclosed by whitewashed 19th-century buildings (including the handsome exterior of the tobacco works, Tinerfeña Fabrica de Tabacos). Begun in 1502, much changed in the 17th and 18th centuries, the church was reopened in 1999 after many years of restoration. The cross which de Lugo first placed on Tenerife soil has been kept here, as has the British flag captured from one of Nelson's ships during the 1797 raid. An additional feature of this fine church is the tomb of Nelson's opponent, General Gutierrez, defender of Santa Cruz.

➕ 35D2
✉ Plaza de la Iglesia
🕐 Daily 9–1, 5:30–8
♿ None
💲 Free
🍴 Nearby in Plaza de la Candelaria (££)

IGLESIA DE SAN FRANCISCO (CHURCH OF ST FRANCIS) ✪✪

This delightful church combines simplicity with elaborate, abundant decoration. Most striking are the wooden ceiling, a painted arch, a fine organ and two baroque *retablos* (altarpieces) dating from the 17th and 18th centuries. To the right of the high altar is a separate chapel with a Moorish-style ceiling. The church, built in 1680, was originally part of the Franciscan monastery of San Pedro de Alcántara, said to have been founded by Irish refugees fleeing from Elizabeth I's anti-Catholic tyranny. The monastery no longer exists, but the buildings now house the Municipal Fine Arts Museum (➤ 37); the square in which it stands was once the friary garden.

➕ 35C3
✉ Calle Villalba Hervás
🕐 Mon–Fri 9–1, 5:30–8
♿ None
💲 Free
🍴 Café del Príncipe (£–££) in Plaza del Príncipe
↔ Museo Municipal de Bellas Artes (➤ 37)

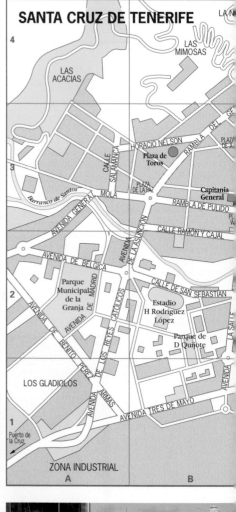

SANTA CRUZ DE TENERIFE

LAS MIMOSAS

LAS ACACIAS

Barranco de Santos

HORACIO NELSON

RAMBLA DEL GE

Plaza de Toros

PLAZA DE JU

CALLE SALAMANCA

PLAZA DE LA PAZ

MOLA

Capitania General

RAMBLA DE PULIDO

AVENIDA GENERAL

AVENIDA DE LA ASUNCIÓN

CALLE RAMÓN Y CAJAL

PL W E

AVENIDA DE BÉLGICA

CALLE DE SAN SEBASTIÁN

Parque Municipal de la Granja

AVENIDA DE MADRID

Estadio H Rodríguez López

AVENIDA DE LOS REYES CATÓLICOS

Parque de D Quijote

AVENIDA

AVENIDA DE BENITO PÉREZ

LA SAITE

LOS GLADIOLOS

AVENIDA ARMAS

AVENIDA TRES DE MAYO

Puerto de la Cruz

ZONA INDUSTRIAL

A   B

Above: *the massive Monumento de los Caidos in Plaza de España, set against the Palacio Insular*

Right: *the Plaza de la Candelaria, a popular pedestrianised shopping area in Santa Cruz*

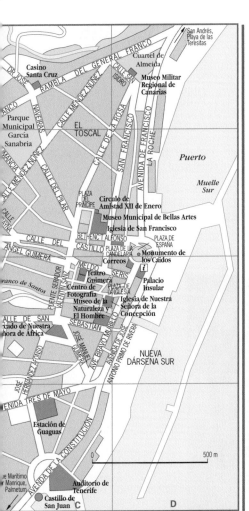

Map labels:

San Andrés, Playa de las Teresitas

Casino Santa Cruz

RAMBLA DEL GENERAL FRANCO

DR. JOSE NAVEIRAS

CALLE MENDEZ NUÑEZ

CALLE SAN ISIDRO

Cuartel de Almeida

Museo Militar Regional de Canarias

CALLE DE LA ROSA

SAN FRANCISCO

AVENIDA DE FRANCISCO LA ROCHE

Parque Municipal García Sanabria

EL TOSCAL

MANCHA

CALLE MENDEZ NUÑEZ

CALLE DEL PILAR

Puerto

Muelle Sur

PLAZA DEL PRINCIPE

Círculo de Amistad XII de Enero

Museo Municipal de Bellas Artes

Iglesia de San Francisco

CALLE DEL
ANGEL GUIMERÁ

CALLE DEL
CASTILLO

BETHENCOURT ALFONSO

PLAZA DE LA CANDELARIA

IMELDO SERIS

Correos

PLAZA DE ESPAÑA

Monumento de los Caídos

Teatro Guimerá

Centro de Fotografía

Museo de la Naturaleza y El Hombre

PUENTE SERRIDOR

VALENTIN SANZ

PLAZA DE LA IGLESIA

SERIS

Palacio Insular

Iglesia de Nuestra Señora de la Concepción

franco de Santos

CALLE DE SAN
rcado de Nuestra
ñora de África

SEBASTIAN

JOSE MANUEL GUIMERÁ

AV. BRAVO MURILLO

AVENIDA DE JOSE

ANTONIO PRIMO DE RIVERA

NUEVA DÁRSENA SUR

JOSE HERNANDEZ ALFONSO

VENIDA TRES DE MAYO

Estación de Guaguas

AVENIDA DE LA CONSTITUCIÓN

0   500 m

ue Marítimo
r Manrique,
Palmetum

Auditorio de Tenerife

Castillo de San Juan

C   D

Above: *a park-bench discussion beneath an elaborate fountain in central Santa Cruz*

Left: *busts adorn the exterior of the Museo Municipal de Bellas Artes, in Plaza del Príncipe*

Around Santa Cruz

Distance
3km

Time
1 hour walking, plus 2 hours
sightseeing

Start/end point
Plaza de España
➕ 35D3

Lunch
Café del Príncipe (££)
✉ Plaza del Príncipe
☎ 922 278810

Start in the waterfront Plaza de España (➤ 40), dominated by its Civil War memorial and the massive Palacio Insular, in which the tourist office and Tenerife's council authorities (Cabildo) are housed.

Walk into the adjoining square, Plaza de la Candelaria.

This agreeable pedestrianised square (➤ 40) has good bars, craft shops and sights, including the Banco Español de Credito in the charming 18th-century Palacio de Carta.

At the end of the square, continue on Calle del Castillo.

This is the main shopping street of Santa Cruz, a lively, colourful avenue of little shops with gaudy signs, 'bazaars' and mingled crowds of tourists and locals.

Continue to Plaza de Weyler.

There's an Italian white marble fountain at the centre of this popular square. To one side stands the Capitanía General, where Franco lived while he was based here.

At the northern tip of the square, turn along Calle Méndez Núñez.

This less interesting street soon leads to the Parque Municipal García Sanabria (➤ 39), an enjoyable green space away from street noise where you can relax on the tiled benches.

Take Calle del Pilar, opposite the park's south side. Follow this street to Plaza del Príncipe.

In the slightly raised square, once the friary garden of a Franciscan monastery, luxuriant laurel trees shade a bandstand. To one side the Municipal Fine Arts Museum (➤ 37) occupies the former monastery, alongside its church, the Iglesia de San Francisco (➤ 33).

Calle de Béthencourt leads the short distance back to Plaza de España.

An opportunity to rest in the shade at Parque Municipal García Sanabria

36

MERCADO DE NUESTRA SEÑORA DE ÁFRICA
(► 23, TOP TEN)

MUSEO MILITAR REGIONAL DE CANARIAS
(CANARIES REGIONAL MILITARY MUSEUM)

Todo por la Patria – All for the Fatherland – is the inscription above the gateway into this collection of important relics from the military past of the Canary Islands. Housed in part of the semicircular 19th-century barracks, Cuartel de Almeida, the museum is proud and patriotic in tone. The oldest exhibits are the simple weapons used by the Guanches against the Spanish. Among various later insignia and memorabilia, a highlight of the collection is El Tigre, the cannon used to defend Santa Cruz against Nelson's 1797 attack and believed to be responsible for the loss of his right arm. Flags taken from one of Nelson's defeated ships, HMS *Emerald*, are also displayed. Even more compelling is the small section devoted to General Francisco Franco, dictator of Spain from 1936 to 1975. You can see his desk, plans and a photograph of Franco with supporters pledging allegiance at Las Raíces, near La Esperanza. A map shows the route of the plane *Dragon Rapide,* which flew from Croydon in southern England to Tenerife, picked up the future dictator and took him to Morocco, from where he launched his coup.

- 35D4
- Calle San Isidro 2
- 922 271658
- Tue–Sun 10–2
- Few
- Free
- Parque Municipal García Sanabria (► 39)
- Remember to take your passport to the Muséo Militar – you probably won't be admitted without it!

El Tigre is famed as the cannon that destroyed Nelson's right arm

MUSEO MUNICIPAL DE BELLAS ARTES
(MUNICIPAL FINE ARTS MUSEUM)

It comes as a surprise, perhaps, that Tenerife's excellent Municipal Fine Arts Museum was opened in 1900, long before the tourism boom. Together with the city library, it is housed in the pleasant setting of a former Franciscan monastery. The 10 busts lined up outside are of Tenerife artists, musicians, writers and thinkers. Inside, the collection on two storeys includes the work of Canarian artists, several of historical interest, and more distinguished European works mainly covering the 17th–19th centuries. Most interesting are the frequent temporary exhibitions of art works loaned by Spain's leading museums of art.

- 35C3
- Calle José Murphy 12, Plaza del Príncipe
- 922 244358
- Mon–Fri 10–8
- Few
- Free
- Café del Príncipe (££)
- Iglesia de San Francisco (► 33)

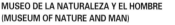

🗺 35C2
✉ Calle Fuente Morales
☎ 922 209320
🕐 Tue–Sun 10–8
♿ Good
🎨 Moderate (Sun free)
🍴 Nearby in Plaza de la
  Candelaria
🔄 Iglesia de Nuestra Señora
  de la Concepción (▶ 33)

MUSEO DE LA NATURALEZA Y EL HOMBRE ✪✪✪
(MUSEUM OF NATURE AND MAN)

This worthy museum, situated in a most attractive former hospital with a galleried courtyard, deals seriously but accessibly with the archaeology, anthropology and ethnography of the Canary Islands, as well as the natural history. The museum is essentially two museums in one – Nature and Man being dealt with separately – and is split in half, naturally following the plan of the building. Archaeology and the history of the Canaries lie on the left of the entrance and the fauna and flora of the islands on the right. Ten distinct sections tackle these different aspects of the Canary Islands with displays as varied as African and pre-Columbian art, aboriginal therapy, the Canaries during the Spanish Conquest and the Canary Islands today.

The main emphasis is placed on the islands' pre-Hispanic history and culture. Much of the evidence of Guanche culture relates to burial, and the museum displays fascinating material from Guanche tombs and burial sites. Some dramatic exhibits include Guanche preserved bodies in a display on mummification, as well as skeletons and hundreds of skulls, some of them trepanned (with drilled holes). Interesting too, though less dramatic, are the displays of Guanche household items, pottery, tools and body decorations, as well as indigenous Canarian plant and animal life.

Above: the attractive courtyard of the Museo de la Naturaleza y el Hombre

🗺 35C1
✉ Avenida de la Constitución
☎ 922 202995
🕐 Daily 10–7
🚌 909 and others along
  Avenida de la Constitución
♿ Good
🎨 Moderate
🍴 Choice on site (£–£££)
🔄 Mercado Nuestra Señora
  de África (▶ 23)

PARQUE MARÍTIMO CÉSAR MANRIQUE ✪✪✪
(CÉSAR MANRIQUE MARINE PARK)

When the Cabildo (Island Council) of Tenerife wanted to do something with the unsightly disused industrial dockyards near the old Castillo de San Juan, they commissioned the brilliant Canarian artist and designer César Manrique to create something for them.

Manrique belived that tourism would be the salvation of the Canary Islands if carefully controlled, but could ruin the islands if given free rein. At Santa Cruz his brief was limited, but even so Manrique managed to redesign the docklands site into an attractive leisure complex linking the sea with the Castillo.

The Castillo itself dates back to 1641, and was part of the town's defences (the Castillo San Cristóbal was located where the Plaza de España lies now). It was once a marketplace for African slaves.

Today the Parque Marítimo is a delightful lido, with palms and sunbathing terraces around a beautiful seawater pool (similar to the Lago Martiánez César Manrique created for Puerto de la Cruz, ► 60).

To the east of the fort lies the town's new Auditorio. Designed like a sea-shell by Santiago Calatrava, it is Santa Cruz's main concert hall. Southwards stretches a huge palm park (Palmetum), still being planted, while across the busy coastal highway is a large, eye-catching exhibition space for trade fairs and conferences.

Below: *Parque Marítimo César Manrique features an imaginative swimming pool*

PARQUE MUNICIPAL GARCÍA SANABRIA ✪✪

This delightful 6-ha park full of shrubs, trees, exotic flowers, fountains and tranquil corners is the largest – and probably the most beautiful – urban park in the Canaries. Popular with locals, it was laid out in the 1920s and is named after the mayor of that time. He is honoured by a large monument in the centre of the park.

The somewhat incongruous pieces of modern sculpture are the product of an international street sculpture competition held in 1973. There is also a zoo, a play area and an intriguing floral clock. Take a break on the tiled benches, stroll the gravel pathways or get a snack at one of the little kiosks.

✚ 35C3
✉ Off Rambla del General Franco
🚌 Town buses along Rambla del General Franco
♿ Good (but gravel paths)
🎟 Free
🍴 Snacks available at park kiosks (£)
↔ Museo Municipal de Bellas Artes (► 37), Iglesia de San Francisco (► 33)

PLAZA DE ESPAÑA

✪✪

35D3
Off Avenida de José Antonio Primo de Rivera
Bars and cafés nearby (£–££)
Plaza de la Candelaria (➤ beow)

A large square near the waterfront, this spacious plaza is the heart of the city. The whole square was formerly the site of the principal Santa Cruz fortification, Castillo San Cristóbal, demolished in 1929. Here now stands the grimly imposing Franco-era Palacio Insular, seat of the Cabildo or Island Council, built in what was known as Rationalist style. The huge central Monumento de los Caidos, Monument to the Fallen, honours local people who fell in war, including the Spanish Civil War – Franco's manifesto was broadcast from here. The monument is flanked by statues of two *menceys* (chieftains).

PLAZA DE LA CANDELARIA

✪✪

35D3
West of Plaza de España
Bars and cafés in the square (£–££)
Iglesia de San Francisco (➤ 33)

This pleasant traffic-free square has good bars and shops, including an *artesanía* (craft shop). Centuries ago, it was the entrance to the vanished Castillo San Cristóbal, once one of the two main defences of the town (the other was Castillo San Juan), and here the island's troops would parade and be inspected. The centrepiece of the plaza is the appealing baroque statue of Our Lady of Candelaria, holding the infant Jesus and a tall candle. Formerly known as Plaza del Castillo, the square acquired its new name along with the statue.

At No 9, the Banco Español de Credito occupies the old Palacio de Carta: behind a rather dull façade this is a fine 18th-century mansion with carved wooden balconies and an elegant patio, immaculately restored by the bank. Originally built as the family home of Captain Matías Carta, it is now one of the best examples of traditional Canarian domestic architecture. Open during bank hours, it deserves a look inside – perhaps when you need to change money.

A statue on Monumento de los Caidos

What to See in the North

BAJAMAR ✪

One of the oldest resorts on Tenerife, Bajamar is a sharp contrast with the glitzier newcomers on the sunny south coast and has a loyal following. Here on the extreme northern shores of the island, constant breezes and turbulent currents stir up the waves onto the black beach. For that reason bathers rarely venture into the sea. Instead, visitors do most of their swimming and sunbathing at the seashore lido and hotel pools. It's also a quieter, less crowded, less developed holiday environment – precisely what attracts its devotees. Once a fishing village, Bajamar has few signs of its past, and now seems unfocused, with a long promenade and side turns, with many bars, restaurants and shops.

🟦 29E5
✉ 15km northwest of La Laguna
🚌 105 (Santa Cruz–Bajamar) every 30 mins
🍴 Variety of bars and restaurants (£–££)
↔ Puntsa del Hidalgo (➤ 50), La Laguna (➤ 45)

Above: *safe inside the saeshore swimming pool at Bajamar*

CASA DE CARTA (➤ 24, TOP TEN)

CASA DEL VINO LA BARANDA ✪✪

Usually known simply as the Casa del Vino, this superb *bodega* (wine cellar) situated in a converted 17th-century farmhouse makes an enjoyable and educational outing – and a great excuse to stock up on a few bottles of local wine. Payment of a small charge enables visitors to taste any 10 of the 150 wines stocked here. Not simply a shop, it sets out to inform tourists about the range and qualities of Tenerife wines.

For those who want to go deeper into the subject, the building houses a small wine museum. It also shows a 10-minute film on the history of wine-making on the island, and explains why here, as in many other wine regions, quality has much improved in recent years. The restaurant (open to all) has panoramic views as well as good food.

🟦 29D4
✉ 1km from Autopista del Norte, at Km 21 (Exit 13, El Sauzal)
☎ 922 572535
🕐 Tue–Sat 11–8, Sun and hols 11–6 (wine tastings until 10)
🍴 Restaurant on site (££) ☎ 922 563388
🚌 101 Puerto–Santa Cruz; 012 from La Laguna
♿ Few
🅿 Free (charge for tastings)
↔ El Sauzal (➤ 44)

41

In the Know

If you only have a short time to visit Tenerife and would like to get a real flavour of the island, here are some ideas:

10

Ways to Be a Local

Order a *caña* – not a *cerveza* or *biera* or beer. Best of all, ask for a Dorada, the locally brewed beer.

Ignore the menu In an ordinary restaurant or bar, locals often don't look at the menu – they just ask the waiter what's on offer that day.

Drink espresso If you want an espresso ask for a *solo*, but for those who prefer a little milk order a *cortado*. It's acceptable, however, to have *café con leche* for breakfast.

Take the kids Locals have a simple answer to the babysitter problem – anywhere that a man can take his wife, he can take his kids. Spanish couples take children with them almost everywhere, at almost any time of day or night. There's no bedtime.

Eat *tapas* – but not before midday. *Tapas* are appetisers or between-meals savouries, and should be nibbled with an apéritif during the long, long hours between lunch and dinner.

Eat late Although Canarian mealtimes are not as late as on the mainland, locals often eat lunch at 2PM and dinner at 9PM.

Take a siesta Locals have a long day, with an early start and a late finish. The secret is to slow down after lunch. Draw the curtains, sit quietly and don't leave your room.

Shout Yell every word. In Spanish, of course.

Hold your drink Get tipsy, laugh, talk loudly, be happy after a few glasses of wine – but uncontrolled, rowdy or drunken behaviour is strictly for tourists.

Forget flamenco Big tourist hotels and other venues put on popular Spanish folklore shows for guests, but traditions like flamenco are not part of Canarian culture.

5

Top Activities

Dive ► 112
Whale-watch ► 107, 111
Golf ► 112
Walk ► 113
Go bananas ► 55

10

Good Places to Have Lunch

Casa del Vino La Baranda (££) Autopista del Norte, km 21 (El Sauzal) 922 572535
Enjoy excellent *tapas* and island wines on the terrace of this delightful 17th-century country house – now a wine museum and showroom.

Chez Arlette (£) La Piedra, Masca 922 863459
Spectacular views over the Masca gorge make this simple place ever-popular with visitors to the Teno Massif in northwest Tenerife.

El Monasterio (££) La Montañeta, Los Realejos 922 320707
In the hilly countryside

Below: dedicated golfers increasingly choose Tenerife for holidays

behind Puerto de la Cruz, this charming place is set in a former convent. Rustic dining rooms ramble through the building, leading to sunny terraces beyond.

Jardín Tecina Restaurant (££) Lomada de Tecina, Playa de Santiago, La Gomera ☎ 922 145850
Enjoy lunch with a superb sea view on this wonderful hotel terrace on the south coast of La Gomera.

La Langostera (£–££) Paseo Maritimo, Los Abrigos ☎ 922 170302
A tempting little fish restaurant where you can enjoy the freshest of simple Canarian cooking.

Las Rocas (£££) Calle Gran Bretaña, Costa Adeje ☎ 922 750100
The beach club of the Hotel Jardín Tropical provides one of the most enjoyable lunchtime experiences on the south coast. Cuisine is high-quality seafood.

Los Troncos (££) Calle General Goded 17, Santa Cruz ☎ 922 284152
One of the best restaurants in the Tenerife capital, noted for its high standard of Canarian cooking and also for its Basque specialities.

Parador de la Gomera (££–£££) Llano de la Horca, San Sebastián, La Gomera ☎ 922 871100
La Gomera's nicely situated *parador* (1km from San Sebastián) has a stylish dining room and the best food on the island. Excellent Spanish and international cuisine.

Parador de las Cañadas del Teide (££) Parque Nacional del Teide ☎ 922 386415
The *parador* restaurant is unpretentious, offers good food and is the nearest to Pico del Teide and the major volcanic sites.

Restaurante El Sombrerito (£) Calle Santa Catalina 15, Vilaflor ☎ 922 709052
In Chicho and Ana's simple village restaurant high up towards the Cañadas, enjoy wholesome Tenerife country cooking. There's a farm museum and shop attached.

5

Ways to Stay All Winter

EU citizens may work and reside in the Canaries though you must apply to your local police station for a residency permit after 3 months.

Tout for restaurants The hard-to-find establishments put touts in the street urging passers-by to come and eat. There's a commission on every customer they bring in.

Teach English Locals need English to get on in tourism, but there's a shortage of native English teachers.

Instruct diving/surfing Diving and surfing schools need qualified English-speaking instructors.

Pull pints There's a fast turnover of English- and German-speaking bar staff in all the resorts.

Go to market Toys, jewellery, drawings, sand art – if you can make anything at all, you can sell it at the markets.

5

Top Beaches

El Médano Tenerife's best natural beaches: 3km of pale sands at this small resort.

Los Cristianos The huge improved beaches at this popular south coast resort are very attractive; most have water sports and are protected by breakwaters.

Playa de las Américas, Costa Adeje This huge resort area has many good artificial beaches.

Playa de las Teresitas Beautiful artificial beach just north of Santa Cruz. Uncrowded on weekdays.

Valle Gran Rey The small shingle beaches at La Playa and Vueltas are two of La Gomera's best beaches.

Below: *The sand at Los Cristianos lends itself to sculpture*

✚ 29D5
✉ About 16km north of Puerto de la Cruz
🍴 Many fish restaurants (£–££)
🚌 101 every 30 min. (Puerto de la Cruz–Santa Cruz); 012 from La Laguna
↔ Puerto de la Cruz (▶ 54), La Laguna (▶ 45)

✚ 29D3
✉ About 23km southwest of Santa Cruz, and 3km inland from the coastal highway
🍴 Bars in the town (£)
🚌 120 from Santa Cruz every 30 min.
↔ Candelaria (▶ 49)
❓ Popular carnival first week of Feb; ancient midsummer festival in Jun

Pyrámides de Güímar Parque Etnográfico
✉ Calle Chacona
☎ 922 514510
🕐 Daily 9:30–6
♿ Good
💰 Expensive

Mysterious man-made structures set against the hills at Güímar

EL SAUZAL ✪

This community has pretty terraced gardens and attractive homes, as well as an unusual domed church in Moorish style, the Iglesia de San Pedro. Its greatest attractions are its wine museum (Casa del Vino ▶ 41) and the exceptional coastal view, especially from the Mirador de la Garañona, which gazes along the sheer cliffs dropping into the sea. A little further along the road, Tacoronte is the heart of Tenerife's wine-making area, noted for its *malvasia* (malmsey) vineyards and its two handsome churches.

GÜÍMAR ✪✪

On the border between the green north and the dry south, Güímar lacks charm but is an authentic Tenerife community with few tourists. Up the slope behind the town stand six curious large mounds, the enigmatic Tenerife step pyramids. Ancient Güímar was a place of importance to the Guanches; it's certain that the chieftain at Güímar had high status, for that was still true when Spanish colonists first began to settle here.

First studied in 1990 by Norwegian explorer Thor Heyerdahl, the six rectangular mounds were once deemed to be no more than piles of volcanic stones cleared from nearby fields by the locals. However, Heyerdahl's excavations showed that the structures are carefully built, arranged in large steps, with a smaller staircase climbing to a ceremonial platform on top. They are aligned with the summer and winter solstices, and closely resemble similar structures in Egypt and Mexico. This adds evidence to the theory that the Guanches were Berbers strongly influenced by ancient Egypt, but more tentatively suggests the Canaries were part of a prehistoric transatlantic route.

The pyramid area is now enclosed within an **ethnographic park**, with a visitor centre, Casa Chacona. One pyramid has been restored and visitors can decide for themselves what to make of the mystery, which archaeologists are still studying.

La Laguna

Outwardly unappealing, the island's second city is a big, sprawling town rapidly spreading towards Santa Cruz, which is only 8km away. Like the capital, La Laguna also has a life and an economy that does not depend upon tourism. Many islanders work here, and there's a thriving university, giving the town a lively, youthful Spanish energy.

Shady Plaza del Adelantado, in La Laguna's historic quarter

La Laguna dates back to 1496, when *conquistador* Alonso Fernández de Lugo set it up as the island's capital, which it remained until 1723. The name means The Lagoon, but there is no lagoon here now (the town is properly known as San Cristóbal de la Laguna). The secret of the town is its exquisite historic quarter, where many fine 16th- and 17th-century Renaissance mansions survive.

It is rewarding to take a leisurely walk around the old quarter. To see most of the sights, stroll along Calle Obispo Rey Redondo from Plaza del Adelantado to Iglesia de Nuestra Señora de la Concepción (▶ 25), and back along parallel Calle San Agustín.

AYUNTAMIENTO (TOWN HALL) ✪

At the start of Calle Obispo Rey Redondo, La Laguna's town hall or *ayuntamiento* is a charming building in Tenerife style. Originally constructed in the 16th century, it was rebuilt in 1822 with fine wooden panelling and a Moorish-style window. Inside, murals illustrate key events from the island's past, and the flag Alonso Fernández de Lugo placed on Tenerife soil has been displayed here.

Next door, Casa de los Capitánes Generales (House of the Captain Generals), built in 1624, is the impressive residence of the island's military commanders. Now it is used as an exhibition space.

> ### DID YOU KNOW?
>
> The Canary Islands are the most westerly part of the European–African land mass, and have always been (and are still today) a last staging post for transatlantic sailors waiting for a good wind before setting off. Thor Heyerdahl's theory, supported by some academics and archaeologists, is that the Guanches belonged to a people from the Middle East, who travelled in reed boats to the Canaries and onward from there to South America.

✚ 29E5
✉ Calle Obispo Rey Redondo
ℹ Plaza del Adelantado
  ☎ 922 631194
 In Plaza del Adelantado (£)

The attractive dome and upper façade of La Laguna's cathedral

Calle San Agustín
In Plaza del Adelantado (£)

CALLE SAN AGUSTÍN ✪✪

In this delightful old-fashioned street parallel to Calle Obispo Rey Redondo, look out for the Instituto de Canarias Cabrera Pinto (Cabrera Pinto Institute of Canarian Studies), noted for its exquisite traditional patio and handsome bell tower. The fine 17th-century façade next door, of the San Agustín monastery, is an empty shell – the building was destroyed by fire in 1963.

Plaza de la Catedral
Mon–Sat 8–1, 5–7:30. Sun open for Mass only
Free

CATEDRAL ✪

The town's large cathedral is older than it appears. Founded in 1515, it was subsequently enlarged and a neoclassical façade was added in 1813. This last feature survives but the remainder was radically rebuilt during the early 20th century. Nevertheless the dim interior contains a gilded baroque retable *(retablo)*, while set back from the high altar is the unostentatious tomb of the island's conqueror and the town's founder, Alonso Fernández de Lugo, buried here in 1525.

Plaza del Adelantado
Mon–Sat 7–11:45, Sun 6:30–8
Free
In Plaza del Adelantado (£)

IGLESIA CONVENTO SANTA CATALINA ✪

The latticework gallery of the Santa Catalina Convent Church, beside the town hall, is one of several attractive architectural features. Inside, the former convent church has a silver-covered altar and baroque *retablos*. Notice the little revolving hatch near the side entrance in Calle Dean Palahi, used by mothers who once wished to abandon their newborn girl babies by 'donating' them anonymously to the convent, to be brought up as nuns.

IGLESIA DE NUESTRA SEÑORA DE LA CONCEPCIÓN
(► 25, TOP TEN)

MUSEO DE LA CIENCIA Y EL COSMOS
(MUSEUM OF SCIENCE AND THE COSMOS)

This fascinating and entertaining museum sets out to show the connection between man and the Earth, and between the Earth and the rest of the universe. With a variety of hands-on exhibits and displays, visitors learn about galaxies, our solar system and the human body, complete with such diversions as listening to the sound of a baby in the womb, taking a lie-detector test and watching a skeleton ride a bicycle.

✉ Calle Vía Láctea, off the La Cuesta road, near the university
☎ 922 315265
🕐 Tue–Sun 9–8:30 (shorter hours in winter)
♿ Few
🎟 Moderate (Sun free)

MUSEO DE HISTORIA DE TENERIFE
(MUSEUM OF TENERIFE HISTORY)

The Casa Lercaro on Calle San Agustín is a grandiose 16th-century colonial mansion, and is the ideal setting for this impressive treasurehouse of island history. The house itself deserves a visit, and anyone really wanting to get a vivid overview of Tenerife's story since the arrival of the Spanish should certainly stop by for a couple of hours at this excellent museum. The collections include historical maps and maritime exhibits, and displays that take the story right up to the present.

✉ Calle San Agustín 22
☎ 922 825949
🕐 Tue–Sun 9–8:30
♿ Few
🎟 Cheap

Below: *exhibits featuring local life in Museo de Historia de Tenerife*

PLAZA DEL ADELANTADO

The heart of old La Laguna is a pleasant, shaded square where locals relax on benches enclosed by some of the most striking historic and dignified buildings in town, including the Ayuntamiento (➤ 45) and the Santa Catalina church (➤ 46) – as well as beautiful mansions adorned with fine porches and balconies. There are bars here too, and the town's busy Mercado Municipal (main market), with its lattice gallery, is the place to join locals in the morning stocking up with fruit and vegetables.

✉ Mercado Municipal, Plaza del Adelantado
☎ 922 258774
🕐 Mon–Sat 8–1
🍴 *Tapas* bars around the square (£)

*Above: looking down to
Santa Cruz from Las
Mercedes in the Anaga
Mountains*

48

LES MONTAÑAS DE ANAGA   ✪✪✪
(ANAGA MOUNTAINS)

Tenerife's northern range of soaring, wild mountains
remains remarkably unspoiled and is an ideal region for
rambling and exploring well off the beaten track. Narrow,
twisting roads give access to dramatic landscapes, while
for walkers it is still possible to see villages reached only
on rough tracks. Here a simple subsistence life continues
without any modern conveniences.

Long-distance paths have been waymarked by ICONA,
the Spanish conservation agency. The ICONA signposting
is clear, so you're not likely to get lost. However, it is
unwise to walk without a detailed map. Walking maps can
be obtained at the Puerto de la Cruz and Santa Cruz tourist
offices and guided walks through the Anaga region can be
organised. There is also an information centre at the
Mirador Cruz del Carmen, where maps and pamphlets
giving details of set walks are available.

Part of the region has been designated a protected
area, the Parque Rural de Anaga. Yet though impressive
and steep, the peaks are not high – Taborno, the highest
point, reaches only 1,024m, and a road follows the crests,
giving superb views from a string of *miradores* (➤ 93,
panel). However, the exposed northern terrain is
often misty, wet or even lightly snow covered on winter
days.

MUSEO DE ANTROPOLOGÍA, CASA DE CARTA
(➤ 24, TOP TEN)

NUESTRA SEÑORA DE LA CANDELARIA, BASÍLICA DE ⭐⭐

The Basilica of Our Lady of Cadelaria is dedicated to the patron saint of the Canary Islands. Profoundly revered, she is always depicted holding the Child in her right arm and a candle in her left hand. Spiritually, her role is as the symbolic bringer of Christian light to the darkness of Guanche life, and so she represents the rightness and justice of the Spanish occupation of the islands.

The legend told by early Spanish settlers – not by the Guanches – was that over a century before the arrival of the first Spanish *conquistadores* the Guanches found a statue of the Virgin and Child set up in a seaside cave. A multitude of legends claim the statue worked miracles to prevent the Guanches from harming her, and that the overawed Guanches began to worship the figure, which they called Chaxiraxi. In a mix of fact and fancy, it is related that the *mencey* (chieftain) of the Guanches welcomed the Spanish at this spot, but that the Guanches were already Christians when the conquerors arrived.

The huge modern Basílica de Nuestra Señora de la Candelaria (1958), set back from the sea, dominates the small town. Inside, the statue of the Virgin sits enthroned in a glorious gilt setting behind the altar, among devotional murals.

The statue dates from about 1830 – what became of the Guanches' Chaxiraxi (which may have looked quite different from today's Virgin) is the stuff of myth. Even before the Spanish arrived in Tenerife, a European living on Fuerteventura is said to have stolen the Guanche statue, but replaced it. Either the original, or its copy, was damaged by fire in 1789 and repaired or replaced. That statue was washed out to sea and lost in 1826, being replaced by the present version a few years later.

In the big sea-facing plaza outside stand sturdy, dignified, sad statues, representing the Guanche chiefs who were the rulers of the island before the coming of the Spanish.

✚ 29E3
✉ On the coast 17km south of Santa Cruz, Plaza de la Basílica, Candelaria
🕐 Daily 7:30–1, 3–7:30
♿ Few
💷 Free
🍴 Bars and restaurants in the town centre (£–£££)
🚌 122, 123, 124, 127, 131 from Santa Cruz
🔄 Santa Cruz (▶ 32)
❓ Festival of the Virgin of Candelaria 14–15 Aug, celebrated throughout the Canary Islands

The much-venerated statue of the Virgin of Candelaria

PLAYA DE LAS TERESITAS ✪✪✪

Despite its huge popularity, the appeal of Tenerife pre-dates the sun, sea and sand recipe of today's mass tourism. Most beaches are unattractive and consist of rough, dark volcanic material (which comes as a shock to some visitors). However, island authorities are aware of the lack and have created some artificial beaches. By far the most outstanding of these is the beautiful curve of Las Teresitas, created in the 1970s with 98,000cu. m of sand from the Sahara desert. Ironically, it was created not in the tourist heartland of the south, but in the far north, where locals could enjoy it. San Andrés, at one end of the beach, is a working fishing village.

✚ 29F5
✉ San Andrés, 8km north of Santa Cruz
🍴 Bars and fish restaurants in San Andrés (£–££)
🚌 910 from Santa Cruz; 246 (Santa Cruz–Almaciga) stops 3 or 4 times daily
♿ Few
↔ Santa Cruz (►32), Anaga Mountains (►48)

The delightful beach at Playa de las Teresitas

PUNTA DEL HIDALGO ✪

If you want to stay at a Tenerife holiday resort yet get away from it all and remain far from the crowds, come to Punta del Hidalgo. Located at the end of a small road on the rocky Hidalgo headland that projects into the Atlantic from the northern coast, it's exposed to wild seas and strong winds. The resort does have its following – it's popular with German visitors and well known as a good place to enjoy the sunset. Its hotels give a fine view over the sea and nearby Anaga Mountains. Most visitors make little use of the sea, preferring to relax at hotel pools. Nevertheless, the resort is growing and gradually extending towards its similar neighbour, Bajamar (►41).

✚ 29E5
✉ 20km north of La Laguna
🍴 Several bars and restaurants in the resort (£–££)
🚌 105 (Santa Cruz–Punta del Hidalgo) every 30 min.
♿ Few
↔ Bajamar (►41), La Laguna (►45), Anaga Mountains (►48)

Northern Hills

Allow a full day to explore the mountainous northern reaches of the island. This is the part which is paradoxically both the most and the least developed, with big working towns on the coast and in the valleys, simple hamlets scattered across the upper slopes, and breathtaking panoramic views from the hill crests. Begin the drive at Santa Cruz, or join at Tacoronte or at any point on the route if coming from the west or south.

Distance
90km

Time
4 hours

Start/end point
Santa Cruz
✚ 29E4

Lunch
Mirador Cruz del Carmen (££)

Head north for 8km on the coastal highway to San Andrés and the Playa de las Teresitas (▶ 50). Turn inland for 10km on TF112, the twisting, climbing road to Mirador El Bailadero.

You're now climbing into the Anaga Mountains (▶ 48). El Bailadero is a magnificent viewpoint, with sweeping vistas of mountain and coast.

Take the high cumbre *(ridge or crest) road, TF1123, towards Mount Taborno. At the fork after 7km, take the summit road.*

A succession of views along this high road includes Mount Taborno's spectacular Mirador Pico del Inglés (a few metres up a side turn on the left). Continue along the crest road, with more viewpoints, notably at Cruz del Carmen, where there is a 17th-century chapel and a restaurant.

After Las Mercedes take the right turn at Las Canteras on TF121 to Tejina. At Tejina, follow TF122 as it turns left towards Tacoronte. 7km beyond Tejina, 1km after Valle de Guerra, pause at the Casa de Carta.

Far-reaching views from Mirador Pico del Inglés

The island's remarkable Anthropology Museum is set in the Casa de Carta (▶ 24), a restored 17th-century farmhouse. Continue on this road to Tacoronte, the wine town (▶ 44).

Leave town on the eastbound autopista *to return to Santa Cruz.*

The West

If the island is divided into two, north and south, then western Tenerife certainly belongs to the north – it is luxuriant, full of colour, life and history. Yet even so the west is something different. Here, away from the busy valleys and towns of the northern peninsula, there is a sense of space and distance and a remoteness from Spain. The climate is hotter and drier, the land more visibly volcanic, the atmosphere more serene. The dominant feature is Pico del Teide, rising far above all else.

Tenerife's first tourists were drawn to Puerto de la Cruz, and smaller resorts formed to either side of it, clinging to the rocky shores, eventually turning the corner at the Macizo de Teno (Teno Massif) and heading down into the south. Those early holidaymakers belonged to a more refined age, and even today the western resorts retain a calmer, less unruly air and attract a more discerning crowd.

> *'Doth not a Tenarif or higher Hill*
> *Rise so high like a Rocke, that one*
> *might thinke*
> *The floating Moone would*
> *shipwracke there and sinke?'*

JOHN DONNE
The First Anniversary (1611)

———————•———————

The rock pools (formed by cooling lava) on Garachico's seafront are ideal for swimming

Puerto de la Cruz

Simply 'Puerto' to old hands, Puerto de la Cruz was the first town on Tenerife to attract tourists – and for good reason. Ideally placed for both north and south, and yet standing at a distance from the workaday world of Santa Cruz, this historic port has a lovely setting. It made a perfect base for the best of leisurely, civilised sightseeing before the days of 'sun, sea and sand'.

✚ 28C4
ℹ Plaza de Europa 5
☎ 922 386000
🕐 Mon–Fri 9–8, Sat–Sun 9–1

The Port of the Cross (as the name means), built in the 1600s by the settlers at La Orotava, grew into a major port after the eruption that destroyed the harbour at Garachico in 1706. Blessed in every way, Puerto is green and luxuriant, with a delightful setting and an exquisite climate. The town clings to the seashore, the lush Orotava Valley rises gently behind and Pico del Teide is clearly visible beyond. Fortunate Puerto is a vibrant, living community that does not depend only on tourism. Its million visitors a year are among the island's most discerning tourists, and enhance the town's charming, bustling atmosphere. After the advent of mass tourism, the new crowds were bussed south to purpose-built resorts in the sun, allowing old Puerto to keep its air of dignity. At the same time it has adapted to the changing needs of tourism, with numerous quality hotels, good shopping, sophisticated entertainment, a casino, pretty public spaces and the best family attractions on Tenerife. For sunbathers, its lido is one of the most appealing in the Canaries.

What to See in Puerto de la Cruz

BANANERA EL GUANCHE ✪✪✪

Bananera El Guanche is a popular family attraction devoted to the subject of the banana – a truly unusual plant. Bananas are a staple of the island economy though the majority are taken by Spain (the Dwarf Cavendish variety cannot be exported due to EU export regulations).

Both entertaining and informative, Bananera is set in an old banana farm (*bananera* means banana plantation). A video (every 20 min.) explains the method of banana cultivation, an extraordinarily complicated and arduous process. The banana, you are informed, is not a tree, but a plant, and takes 16–19 months before it produces its first 'hand' of bananas. One of its many peculiarities is that each plant is both male and female, and reproduces without pollination.

Visitors then stroll along a route that takes them through various kinds of banana plants, as well as many other intriguing species. You'll see varieties as diverse as papaya, mango, the huge and ancient *drago* (or dragon tree) species, sugar cane, cotton, coffee, cocoa, peanuts, pineapples and more. Less familiar names include kapok and *chirimoya* (custard apples). The cactus garden has hundreds of cacti, while in the Tropical Plantation there is a wide range of fruit trees as well as *datura*, tobacco and *chicle* – the South American tree from whose milky resin chewing gum is derived. There are exotic flowers too, including elegant, vivid *strelitzia*, or bird of paradise flowers, which have become a symbol of the Canary Islands. Boxed *strelitzia* flowers are a popular souvenir for Bananera visitors; they can be delivered to your hotel on the day of your flight home.

Finally, before leaving, you're offered a free taste of banana liqueur (powerful – and sweet) and a ripe banana. Many interesting fruit and flower specimens and souvenirs can be bought in the shop, carefully prepared and packed for the flight home.

DID YOU KNOW?

The first examples of the banana were brought here some five centuries ago from Indo-China, and continued their journey to the newly discovered West Indies. In 1855 a small variety known as the Dwarf Cavendish or the Chinese banana was introduced, which became especially associated with the Canary Islands.

✚ 28C4
✉ 2km from Puerto de la Cruz on the road to La Orotava
☎ 922 331853
🕐 Daily 9–6
♿ Few
👋 Expensive
🍴 Bar on site (£), restaurants in town (£–£££)
🚌 Free bus to Puerto de la Cruz every 20 or 30 min.

Above: *Bananera El Guanche provides an unusual day out for visitors to Puerto de la Cruz*
Opposite: *Puerto's main church stands in Plaza de la Iglesia*

Calle San Juan, off Calle
Iriarte
Mon–Sat 10–7
None
Cheap

Above: *Casa Iriarte, the
birthplace of Tomás de
Iriarte, writer of fables
and translator of Horace*

Paseo de Luis Lavagi
Open for events and
exhibitions
None
Variable
In Calle de San Felipe
(£–££)
Playa Jardín (▶ 61)

CASA IRIARTE

Tomás de Iriarte, born in this house on 18 September
1750, numbers among the very few Tinerfeños to have
made a name for themselves outside the island (▶ 14).
His poetry, plays and essays, and in particular his scholarly
translations (for example, from Latin into German), made
him a distinguished figure in 18th-century Spanish literary
circles. He left the family home at the age of 13 to
continue his education in Madrid, where he remained until
his death in 1791. This house was once considered an
architectural treasure. It has fine traditional carved
balconies and a beautiful interior courtyard, still well worth
seeing, even though the house is today a charmless
souvenir craft shop (one of too many in the area) with a
low-key maritime museum upstairs.

CASTILLO DE SAN FELIPE

A sturdy little coastal fortification, the diminutive Castillo de
San Felipe is named after King Philip IV of Spain (1621–65).
It was during his reign that settlers began to construct
Tenerife's first capital, La Orotava, and its port, Puerto de
la Cruz. The Castillo dates from that period and it remains
the best example in the Canary Islands of the Spanish
colonial style of architecture. The building has been immaculately restored and is now a cultural centre. Classical
concerts are often given here, which provides the option
for visitors of a pleasing change from the usual type of
entertainment on offer. The Castillo also houses art
exhibitions.

ERMITA DE SAN TELMO

San Telmo (St Elmo) is the patron saint of sailors, and the seafarers of Puerto de la Cruz erected this simple waterfront chapel in his honour in 1626 (rebuilt in 1780 after a fire). Its also known as the Capilla de San Telmo (Chapel of St Elmo). Dazzling white but for a tiny bellcote, it stands in a lovely little garden surrounded by the noisy ebb and flow of tourists and traffic. Although the street outside is named after the church, as is a nearby beach, there is something that touches the soul in this humble place. Here fishermen gave thanks for having been spared from the dangers of the ocean, while beneath the floor are buried some who were less fortunate, victims of a flood in 1826.

Calle de San Telmo
Daily. Services Wed, Sat 6:30PM, Sun 9:30, 11AM
Free
Nearby (£–££)

The gardens of San Telmo provide a quiet space alongside modern high-rise buildings

✉ Plaza de la Iglesia

☎ 922 380051

🕐 Mon–Sat 3–7, Sun 9–7.
Mass daily 8:30, 6:30, 7

👋 Free

🍴 Drink or snack on terrace
of Hotel Marquesa, Calle
Quintana 11 (££)

✉ Calle Retama 2, off
Carretera del Botánico

☎ 922 383572

🕐 Summer, daily 9–7;
winter, 9–6

♿ Few

👋 Cheap

🍴 Hotel Botánico (£££); no
casual dress

🚌 Along Carretera del
Botánico

IGLESIA DE NUESTRA SEÑORA DE LA PEÑA DE FRANCIA ✪

Puerto's main church, the Church of Our Lady of the Rock of France, was started in the 1680s and took nearly 20 years to complete – even then it lacked the pale angular bell tower, added as an afterthought some 200 years later. Standing among the tall palms and flowering shrubs near the elegant central fountain (in the shape of a swan) in Plaza de la Iglesia, the church possesses a sombre dignity. The baroque interior is decorated with some fine statuary, as well as an ornate altarpiece by Luis de la Cruz in a side chapel. The organ comes from London – it was ordered and installed in 1814 by Bernardo de Cologán, one of several Canary islanders of Irish origin. Notice, too, the striking pulpit: its wood has been painted to look like marble.

JARDÍN BOTÁNICO (BOTANICAL GARDENS) ✪✪✪

One of the most enjoyable places to pass some time in Puerto is the exuberant, exotic and colourful Botanical Gardens on the edge of town. It's the perfect place to rest out of the sun, grab a cool moment of tranquillity, or enjoy a serene park-bench picnic. Here hundreds of intriguing plant varieties grow in profusion, set in a peaceful shady park of only some 2.5ha. In places, roots, branches and twisting trunks form a fascinating sculptural tangle. Almost everything in the gardens is a native of some other land, the focal point being a huge 200-year-old fig tree, brought here as a sapling from South America. Today it rears up on an astonishing platform of roots. Like the other plants, it has truly flourished in this foreign soil, in an unarguable testimony to the benign climate and conditions of the island.

The gardens were set up in 1788 by King Carlos III as part of an experiment to see if it was possible to acclimatise plants to live in other climate zones. The intention was to see if useful varieties growing in tropical colonies could be 'trained' to survive in the mainland of Spain. The question was reasonable at the time, for it was not known how or why plant species live only in certain parts of the planet. The correct name of the Jardín Botánico to this day is El Jardín de Aclimatación de La Orotava (La Orotava Acclimatisation Garden).

The range of species is prodigious, and includes several hundred plant varieties – some of which can also be seen at the Bananera El Guanche (▶ 55). Pepper trees, breadfruit trees, cinnamon trees and tulip trees mingle with coffee bushes and mango trees. Lovers of exotic flowers

Right and inset: The
Jardín Botánico boasts
a wide variety of exotic
specimens

will be thrilled by the splendid hothouse orchids.

Tropical plants that thrived in these gardens were then taken to similar Royal Gardens at Madrid and Aranjuez in Spain to see whether – after their spell of adapting to the climate in Tenerife – they could 'learn' to survive on the mainland. For most mainland Spain proved simply too cold in winter and the results were broadly unsuccessful. It is now better understood that while some plants can prosper away from home others cannot; for most of the exotics growing in the Jardín Botánico Tenerife was as far as they were willing to travel. Many other varieties that were brought here failed to put down roots even in Tenerife.

📧 Playa Martiánez, Avenida de Colón

📞 922 385955

🕐 Daily 10–7 (last entry 5PM)

♿ Few

💰 Moderate

🍴 Several eating places on site (£–£££)

🚌 Along waterfront

↔ Ermita San Telmo (➤ 57)

LAGO MARTIÁNEZ ✪✪✪

As a traditional resort, Puerto de la Cruz had a major drawback in the new era of mass package tourism: it had no decent beach. The solution was this beautiful lido, designed by the inspirational Lanzarote architect César Manrique and completed in 1977. Manrique was also responsible for the Playa Jardín, also in Puerto de la Cruz, which he developed in 1992 (➤ 61).

In the 1970s, when the town wondered how to respond to the growing demand for swimming and sunbathing facilities, it consulted Manrique, who was based on Lanzarote. An internationally acclaimed modern artist, he had recently returned to his native Canary Islands, where he had been given a free hand to develop tourist attractions.

Manrique had strong views on mass tourism, which he believed could be of great benefit to the Canary Islands, but at the risk of destroying the landscape, local culture and traditional architecture. He argued that tourism should be encouraged within strict controls and that facilities should be of the highest, most creative standard.

Marketed under various names (Costa Martiánez, Lido de San Telmo, Lido de Martiánez), the Lago contains some 27,000cu. m of filtered seawater. It consists of eight attractively shaped pools and a larger swimming lake, inter-

spersed with refreshing fountains and islets of lush greenery; the complex has proved a great success. Waterside sunbathing terraces, shaded by palms, are laid out in white and black volcanic rock.

Touches of art and humour are everywhere: a popular feature is a central lava isle which periodically erupts as a fountain. The summit of Pico del Teide makes a dramatic backdrop inland. Besides several on-site bars and restaurants, there's also a glitzy cabaret show-restaurant called Andromeda at the Isla del Lago.

Left: *Lago Martiánez is deservedly popular with visitors*

LORO PARQUE (➤ 21, TOP TEN)

MUSEO ARQUEOLÓGICO ✪ (ARCHAEOLOGICAL MUSEUM)
Located near the old fishing harbour, this small archaeological museum is housed in an attractive 19th-century building. The collection relates to the ethnography of the Guanche people. Interesting permanent displays include early maps, ceramics, equipment used in farming, jewellery, weapons and information on mummification. The museum hosts temporary exhibitions.

⊠ Calle del Lomo 9A
☎ 922 371465
🕐 Tue–Sat 10–1, 5–9, Sun 10–1
♿ Few
💷 Cheap
🍴 Eating places nearby (£), especially in Calle de San Felipe
↔ Plaza del Charco (➤ 62), Puerto Pesquero (➤ 62)

PLAYA JARDÍN ✪✪
In 1992 the Canarian artist César Manrique transformed the neglected rocky bay near the Castillo de San Felipe into a remarkable waterfront beach garden. Manrique had had earlier success with the Lago Martiánez (➤ opposite), nearer the town centre.

The site was chosen partly because the coast is more sheltered here and has less dangerous currents. Over 20,000cu. m of dark sand were imported to form a glorious stretch of beach, heightened by magnificent gardens of flowering bushes, palms and exotics cultivated on the surrounding sand and rock. Rocks rising inland add a backdrop to the scene.

Thousands of offshore concrete wave breakers hidden beneath the water protect Manrique's beach and gardens from the power of the ocean. As a result, Playa Jardín has become become one of the resort's most popular beaches. It has been awarded a Blue Flag, a symbol of good environmental standards and safety.

⊠ At the western end of town, near Punta Brava
♿ Few
💷 Free
🚌 102, 325, 343, 382 from the resort centre
🍴 In the nearby fishermen's quarter, especially Calle San Felipe (£–££)
↔ Castillo de San Felipe (➤ 56), Loro Parque (➤ 21)

✉ Off Calle Blanco, near the
fishing harbour
🍴 Bars and restaurants in
the square (£–££)
↔ Puerto Pesquero (below)

PLAZA DEL CHARCO ✪✪

A *charco* is a pool or pond, and this animated raised square
stands where once shallow waters collected from the sea
and locals fished for shrimps. Now the plaza, with its
ancient Indian laurel trees, is the very heart of Puerto's old
quarter and full of life – with bars and cafés, buskers and
strollers. The charming restored 18th-century Rincón del
Puerto, on the west side, has traditional balconies and a
courtyard, now occupied by bars.

PUERTO PESQUERO (FISHING HARBOUR) ✪✪

✉ At the end of Calle
Blanco
🍴 In Calle Blanco and Plaza
del Charco (£–££)
↔ Plaza del Charco (see
above)

There's no more picturesque reminder that Puerto does
not exist only for tourists than this small working fishing
harbour, not far from lively Plaza del Charco. A low harbour
wall of black volcanic stone encloses the little bay. Modest
but brightly painted rowing boats are hauled up on the
shore, where local men and boys gather to talk or work.

On one corner, beside the water, a handsome building of
dazzling white paint and bare black stone is the former
Casa de la Real Aduana – the Royal Customs House. Built
in 1620, this small public office continued to function as a
customs house until 1833. (It is not open to the public.)
Behind are 18th-century harbour defences that protected
the town and port from raiders.

Across the street, Casa de Miranda dates from 1730.
It's a fine restored house, once the home of Venezuelan
liberator Francisco Miranda, and now a bar and restaurant
(► 95).

*Fishing boats enliven
the harbour at Puerto
Pesquero*

Around Puerto

Puerto still has an atmosphere of history and much of the central area of this graceful colonial town is pedestrianised.

Start from Plaza de la Iglesia.

This handsome main square, with its palms and a lovely swan fountain, is dominated by the church (► 58).

Take Calle de Cologán (away from the sea) and turn into the second right, Calle Iriarte.

Reaching Plaza Concejil and Calle San Juan, you'll find the elegant balconied 18th-century house Casa Iriarte to the right, now a souvenir and craft shop and a minor naval museum (► 56). On your left is the landmark Palacio Ventosa, with its tall tower.

Continuing along Calle Iriarte , turn right into Calle Blanco.

This brings you to Plaza del Charco, the pleasantly bustling and shaded heart of town (► 62).

Take Calle de San Felipe from the northwest corner of the square.

This street has unpretentious restaurants and traditional Canarian buildings of character. Turn right and right again into Calle de Lomo, for the Museo Arqueológico (► 61).

Retrace your steps to Plaza del Charco, then turn left on Calle Blanco towards the sea.

Here is the Puerto Pesquero (► 62), the endearing little harbour with the modest Casa de la Real Aduana (Royal Customs House) on one corner.

Follow the main seashore road (Calle de Santo Domingo) eastward past Punta del Viento (Windy Point), eventually reaching Calle de San Telmo.

Pause to admire the tiny Ermita de San Telmo (► 57). Continue to the Lago Martiánez (► 60).

Distance
1½km

Time
1½ hours

Start point
Plaza de Iglesia

End point
Lago Martiánez

Lunch
Tapas bars (£–££) and restaurants (££)
✉ Plaza del Charco, Calle de San Felipe

Strolling along the seafront in Calle de San Telmo

What to See in the West

GARACHICO (▶ 20, TOP TEN)

ICOD DE LOS VINOS ★★

One of the highlights of a tour around Tenerife is the little town of Icod. Its main attraction is the gigantic Dragon Tree known – with poetic licence – as the Drago Milenario, the Thousand-Year-Old Dragon Tree (▶ 17). But Icod has other charms too. The Plaza de la Iglesia, apart from its view of the ancient *drago*, has a lovely 15th-century church, the Iglesia de San Marcos, containing a baroque altarpiece, a fine timber ceiling and a magnificent 2m-tall cross from Mexico, a masterpiece of delicate silverwork. A short distance away, the Mariposario del Drago (Butterfly Garden) is aflutter with colourful tropical butterflies.

As the name makes clear, Icod is also known for its wines. Taste and buy them at shops near Plaza de la Iglesia, such as Casa del Vino or Casa del Drago.

✚ 28B4

🍴 Bars and restaurants nearby (▶ 94)

🚌 354, 363 (Puerto de la Cruz–Icod) every 30 min.

↔ Garachico (▶ 20)

❓ Fiestas on 22 Jan, 25 Mar, 24 Jun and 29 Nov; Corpus Christi in Jun; Santa Barbara end Aug; Dragon Tree Festival in Sep

Plaza de la Constitución in Icod de los Vinos, near the Iglesia de San Marcos

MACIZO DE TENO (TENO MASSIF) ★★★

The volcanic basalt mountains in northwestern Tenerife are among the most ancient rocks of the island. Their unusual geology and flora, and the steep, buckled terrain make the Teno Massif a splendid place for hiking.

Masca, a mountain village perched above a deep gorge, was once remote and virtually inaccessible. Now a daringly engineered road has made it a popular excursion, with roadside restaurants providing dazzling views.

Another improved road leads west from the little regional centre of Buenavista del Norte to Tenerife's most westerly point, the Punta de Teno, a dramatic headland with a lighthouse, where the Atlantic breaks against black rocks. Buenavista del Norte itself has a pretty main square with some 18th-century mansions; the church of Nuestra Señora de los Remedios has fine altarpieces and a notable *mudéjar* (Moslem-style) ceiling.

✚ 28A3–A4

🍴 Bars and restaurants in Buenavista del Norte, Los Gigantes (▶ 94)

↔ Los Gigantes (▶ 22)

LA OROTAVA ✪✪✪

Puerto de la Cruz was originally built as the port for older and grander La Orotava, the hilltown just inland whose coat of arms still declares it to be a Villa Muy Noble y Leal (most noble and loyal town). A jewelbox of balconied façades, pretty decoration, cobbled streets and beautifully preserved historic buildings, La Orotava is best explored on foot. Start with the wonderful views from Plaza de la Constitución. The towers and dome of baroque Iglesia de Nuestra Señora de la Concepción in Plaza Casañas are a distinctive landmark.

Calle San Francisco is the highlight, climbing the west side of town from Plaza San Francisco to Plaza Casañas. Casa de los Balcones (➤ 16) is its main attraction. Across the street the **Casa del Turista**, though less grand, is older from about 1590 but in the same style, and has a craft shop where demonstrations are given of making sand pictures, a feature of the town's Corpus Christi celebrations. Also along here, 17th-century Hospital de la Santísima Trinidad used to be a convent – the revolving drum set in the wall by the main door was used to leave unwanted babies to be brought up by the nuns.

Interesting museums in town include **Museo de Artesanía Iberoamericana**, celebrating the artistic and cultural links between Spain (including the Canary Islands) and Latin America; **Casa Torrehermosa** (➤ 109), showcasing the best of the island's arts and crafts; and out-of-town **Museo de Cerámica**, with 1,000 pieces of traditional pottery. All three are housed in beautifully restored historic buildings.

Left: *a macabre painted mask in Museo de Artesanía Iberoamericana*
Above: *the impressive façade of the Liceo de Taoro, a private club in La Orotava*

LOS GIGANTES (➤ 22, TOP TEN)

🞤 28C4
✉ 6km southeast from Puerto de la Cruz
ℹ Carrera Escultor Estévez 2
☎ 922 323041
🍴 Modest restaurants and *tapas* bars in Plaza de la Constitución
🚌 101, 345, 348, 350, 352 from Puerto de la Cruz
↔ Puerto de la Cruz (➤ 54)
❓ Corpus Christi in Jun

Casa del Turista
✉ Calle San Francisco 4
☎ 922 330620
🕐 Mon–Fri 9–7, Sat 8:30–5
♿ None
🎟 Free

Museo de Artesanía Iberoamericana
✉ Calle Tomás Zerolo 34
☎ 922 323376
🕐 Mon–Fri 9–6, Sat 9–2
♿ None
🎟 Moderate

Casa Torrehermosa
✉ Calle Tomás Zerolo 27
🕐 Mon–Fri 9:30–6:30, Sat 9:30–2
🎟 Free

Museo de Cerámica Casa Tafuriaste
✉ 4km west town centre at Calle León 3
☎ 922 321447
🕐 Mon–Sat 10–6, Sun 10–2
🎟 Cheap

Parque Nacional del Teide (Teide National Park)

The Guanche name for Pico del Teide, the immense volcano rising at the heart of the island, was 'Tenerife'. For them, the mountain was the island, though in geological terms that's only partly correct. It was the emergence of this volcano, along with the Anaga and Teno ranges, that created Tenerife and subsequently shaped the island's terrain and dominated its natural and cultural development.

While the northern fringes of the island are fertile and inhabited, the landscape around Pico del Teide remains harsh and unyielding. In particular, the area within the Caldera de las Cañadas, the remnants of a far bigger volcano whose eroded walls enclose Pico del Teide, is an awesome combination of rock and dust. In 1954 the surroundings of Pico del Teide were made a national park, its boundaries roughly following the borders of the caldera. Covering 189sq km, the whole park lies above the 2,000m contour. It is strictly protected from any development.

The park can be visited by car, by coach (especially on through road C821), or by bike or on foot on numerous smaller tracks and paths. A cable car (*teleférico*) runs up Pico del Tiede to a point 163m below the summit (▶ 18). The cable-car station is 4km from the *parador*.

The **visitor centre** at the high El Portillo pass, east of Pico del Teide on the park through road, provides an introduction to the national park. An exhibition and video explains the volcanoes and there is a garden of local flora. For walkers detailed maps of the park are available and excellent free guided walks set out from here (reserve a place by telephoning at least a day ahead). The *parador* too has a small visitor centre and an exhibition.

Above: the giant crater of Caldera de las Cañadas

Western Tenerife

This day out takes in all the grandeur of Tenerife's volcanic heartland.

Leave Puerto de la Cruz on the motorway heading towards Santa Cruz, but exit at junction 11 (Tacoronte) for La Esperanza.

Below: *Driving along the Carretera Dorsal road towards Teide National Park*

La Esperanza is popular for lunch and a walk in the high pine woods of the Bosque de la Esperanza, just south on C824. This road is the Carretera Dorsal running along the mountainous 'spine' of the island (► 68).

Take C824 south from La Esperanza. The road rises through pine woods, often shrouded in clouds or mist.

At a bend, a sign points the way to the Las Raices monument, marking the spot where Franco met army officers to plan their coup. Pause at the Mirador Pico de las Flores and other viewpoints for dramatic views of the north coast. Eventually the road passes the observatory at Izaña and enters the national park (► 66).

Follow C824 to the junction with C821 and follow it to the left, continuing south.

The Centro de Visitantes (► 66), at El Portillo pass, marks the entrance to the Caldera de las Cañadas. After 11km of volcanic terrain you reach the Pico del Teide cable car (► 18) and 4km further, the *parador*, nearly opposite Los Roques de García (► 68).

At Boca del Tauce, the typical Cañadas scenery abruptly ends. Return through the park to the Centro de Visitantes at El Portillo.

Beyond El Portillo, take the left-hand fork down into the Valle de la Orotava, passing through heath, vines and, on the lowest level, bananas.

Continue the descent into Puerto de la Cruz.

Distance
145km

Time
4 hours

Start/end point
Puerto de la Cruz
28C4

Lunch
Restaurants near El Portillo
and the *parador*

67

✚ 28C3–29E5

Los Roques de García form part of the extraordinary volcanic landscape

CUMBRE DORSAL ✪✪✪

Of all the routes to the Teide National Park, the most spectacular is the Carretera Dorsal road (C824), along the crest of the Cumbre Dorsal – the uplands that run northeast from the national park to the Anaga Mountains. Their slopes rise behind the Orotava Valley, with wonderful views to the sides and ahead. Along the road a number of *miradores* make unmissable stopping points (➤ 67).

✚ 28C3

✉ Near C821 just south of the *parador*

🍴 Book at the *parador* (££)
☎ 922 386415.
Restaurant at Boca del Tauce (££) ☎ 922 850529)

🚌 348 once daily each way from Puerto de la Cruz to the *parador*. 342 once daily stops here from Playa de las Américas

🖐 Free

❓ Choose clear, calm weather and come early to avoid the crowds

LAS CAÑADAS ✪✪✪

This spectacular caldera, a crater zone measuring some 16km across, consists of lava fields, sandy plateaux (*cañadas*) and several freakish natural phenomena. One in particular, Los Roques de García, comprises a majestic cluster of misshapen rocks, easily spotted just opposite the *parador*. A waymarked walk goes round the Roques and is planted with various local flowers. To the north looms the awesome peak of Teide itself (➤ 18), while to the south lies the arid, sandy plain known as the Llano de Ucanca.

Another impressive rock formation is Los Azulejos (by the roadside about 1km south of Los Roques de García). This geological curiosity takes its name from the brilliant blue-green colorations of the rocks (*azulejos* is Andalucian for glazed tiles), caused by deposits of iron and copper mineral salts.

✚ 28C3

PAISAJE LUNAR (LUNAR LANDSCAPE) ✪✪

Accessible only on foot, this area of the park is a bizarre visual phenomenon. Here, high in the midst of nowhere, strange columns and shapes of tufa make a weird unearthly landscape. To reach the Lunar Landscape area involves an 11km round trip on marked footpaths just east of the *parador*.

Walk up Pico del Teide

The ascent of Pico del Teide is the most exhilarating walk on Tenerife – though it's only suitable for fit, experienced ramblers. Take plenty of water and warm clothes, and start as early as possible, checking the weather forecast and that the cable car is running for the return journey (► 18).

Start from the main road C821 at the start of the track to Montaña Blanca.

At first the track passes through a desolate volcanic terrain of sharp, gritty stones. After an hour or an hour and a half, you reach the old Montaña Blanca car park.

Follow the sign indicating the Refugio de Altavista, which starts you on a steeper climb on a sandy track. Climb for about 2 hours along this path to reach the refugio, or mountain refuge – which may or may not be open (usually open daily 5PM to 10AM). Continue on the path, the edge of which is clearly marked.

Some 3 hours later, the path becomes stonier, but more level. Eventually you reach the path that leads from the top cable-car station to the summit. To complete the ascent you need a permit (► 19).

In a wild landscape of multicoloured volcanic rock and scree, the path becomes a steep scramble.

You'll pass sulphurous steam holes emitting heat and vapour from the ground. The views are phenomenal. The summit is marked by a crucifix, where sometimes elderly local women come to say a prayer, seemingly climbing here with ease.

Return to the cable-car station and take the car down to the road.

Distance
8km

Time
6–7 hours

Start point
From C821 Montaña Blanca bus stop
✚ 28C3

End point
Top cable-car station (La Rambleta), or the summit
✚ 28C3

Lunch
Take a picnic – no food or water en route. There is a bar at La Rambleta (£).

For advice on easier walks within the national park, call at the Centro de Vistantes (Visitor Centre) at El Portillo (► 66)

Suitably equipped, walkers contemplate the rugged countryside

Food & Drink

With so many popular eateries in the resorts focusing on holiday favourites like pizza, pasta and paella, it's easy to forget that most inland restaurants offer traditional local cuisine, usually in cool, simple, tiled surroundings. Look out for the word *tipico*, meaning roughly 'traditional' or 'local'.

Customers at a typical tapas bar in Puerto de la Cruz

Fish and Vegetables

Tenerife's staple is quality fresh fish. Most popular are *vieja* (parrot or sun fish) and *merluza* (hake), *abade*, *mero* and *cabrilla* (all forms of sea bass) and *cherne* (a larger bass often cut and served in steaks). Fish is usually prepared in a plain and simple way, such as grilled or fried, and served with a dressing of oil, vinegar and mildly hot peppers or *mojo* (see right) together with a vegetable or two. Salted fish is also traditional. Among the vegetables, the most typical and traditional are *papas arrugadas,* or wrinkly potatoes. These delectable salty new potatoes,

Fresh local fish displayed for sale

cooked in their skins with plenty of salt until the water has completely boiled away, are properly served with *mojo*. They are a must, if not good for low-sodium diets, and even on their own make a delicious snack.

Stews

The people of Tenerife are fond of hearty stews, usually combining several meats including pork and rabbit with chickpeas and vegetables and often thickened with *gofio* (see below). *Rancho canario* and *puchero* are typical traditional thick meat stews, popular for Sunday lunch. *Potaje*, vegetable stew, is a less meaty alternative (though vegetarians beware, even this might contain a little meat!). The fishy version is *sancocho*, a thick stew of salted fish and vegetables. Served with bread, such stews can make a complete meal.

Gofio

Nothing is more Canarian than *gofio*, the versatile staple of the native Guanche diet that is still very much in use. A rough roasted wholemeal flour (usually of maize, but possibly also of barley, wheat or even chickpeas), it appears in soups, as a sort of polenta, as a paste mixed with vegetables, or as breads, cakes and puddings.

Produce at a roadside market stall

Mojo

One of the most genuinely Canarian words on the menu is *mojo*. Meat, fish and vegetables may all be served *con mojo*, with mojo, the piquant sauce that comes in different versions, more or less spicy according to what it accompanies. The two main types are *mojo verde*, green mojo, its parsley and coriander recipe giving a cool, sharp flavour, and *mojo rojo*, the spicier, red sauce made with chillis and peppers. Grilled goat's cheese, too, is served *con mojo*.

Local wines

Desserts

Banana flambé is a must in the resorts, but is not so common in authentic local restaurants. *Gofio* is used to make desserts such as the semolina-like *flan gofio*, or popular *frangollo*, which is made of gofio and dried fruit. Syrupy, nutty *bienmesabe* pudding is the Canarians' favourite.

Wine

Tenerife's wines have been drunk in Europe for centuries, traditionally a sweet, rich, heady brew, made from the *malvasia* grape used to make old-fashioned malmsey. Nowadays Tenerife wines can be dry or sweet, red or white. The main wine-growing area is around El Sauzal, just north of Puerto de la Cruz. La Gomera, too, makes drinkable table wine. Make sure you try the sweet dessert wine of Vallehermoso.

The South

The climate that caused Spanish colonists to stay in the green north of the island is the very thing that has caused foreign tourists to flock to the south. Everything beyond the lee of Pico del Teide is bone dry, a land stripped bare by Saharan sun. The light is dazzlingly pure and clear, the hills casting magical views across the emptiness to a perfect blue sea. From centuries this was the least valuable part of the island, in places little more than a desert. Up on the slopes some simple, remote shepherd villages survived, while down on the coast the harbour of Los Cristianos benefited from its sheltered position out of the wind. Now, though, the south is full of life and entertainment. Today that once-empty southern coast harvests Tenerife's most valuable crop: sun-seeking tourists. And for them, there can be no better place to be on this island.

> *'I scarcely ever went out without finding some new wonder to paint, and lived a life of the most perfect peace and happiness.'*
>
> OLIVIA STONE
> *Tenerife and its Six Satellites* (1887)

———————●———————

Puerto Colón marina in the resort of Playa de las Américas

🗺 28B1

✉ Exits 27, 28, 29 or 30 of
Autopista del Sur

🍴 Tourist restaurants
(£–£££) near beaches and
close to Puerto Colón and
Los Cristianos harbour

🚌 111 to Santa Cruz.
Frequent services to all
southern resorts; collect
timtable frrom any tourist
office. TITSA bus
information ☎ 922
531300

Costa Adeje, Los Cristianos and Playa de las Américas

Los Cristianos effectively merges with Playa de las Américas, though it's less brash, more family orientated and has some Spanish character. The heart of Tenerife's package-holiday scene is a round-the-clock resort with a vast choice of accommodation, bars, restaurants and entertainment. Surprisingly, the location is still beautiful, with rocky hills behind and attractions around the edges of town. The area extends westward from Los Cristianos through Playa de las Américas and into the newer district of Costa Adeje.

What to see in Costa Adeje, Los Cristianos and Playa de las Américas

AQUAPARK ✪✪

🗺 28B1

✉ Exit 29 of Autopista del
Sur

☎ 922 715266

🕐 Daily 10–6

♿ Good

💰 Expensive

🍴 On site (£–££)

🚌 Free from southern
resorts

A hugely popular waterpark with pools, rides, slides, flumes, wild water and dolphin displays. Many families, especially those with younger children, prefer to base themselves here throughout their stay.

COSTA ADEJE ✪

🗺 28B1

ℹ Avenida Puig de Lluvina
☎ 922 750633

Extending north from Playa de las Américas and the Playa de Troya, this vast and still-expanding development now extends to La Caleta and beyond. Aiming upmarket, many of its newer hotels are elegant neoclassical designs, with masses of marble, pillars, tiles, lush gardens and state-of-the-art facilities.

Puerto Colón, a smart marina of ocean-going yachts, makes a focal point in this huge and somewhat amorphous resort (► 72).

JARDINES DEL ATLÁNTICO BANANERA ✪

🗺 28B1

✉ Exit 26 of Autopista del
Sur ☎ 922 720360

🕐 Daily 10–6; last admission
4:15 💰 Expensive

🍴 On site (££)

🚌 Free from southern
resorts

Though a second best to the Bananera attraction in Puerto de la Cruz (► 55), this one offers an opportunity to see, taste and learn about bananas in a genuine banana farm. You'll also learn lots of other things about Tenerife, including its crops and wild plants, and how Pico del Teide distributes the rainwater that falls on the island. There are guided tours round the gardens.

LOS CRISTIANOS ● ● ●

As this was the only coastal town already in existence in the late 1960s, when sun-seekers arrived in the south, it was to this harbour that they came. Los Cristianos already had a few bars and a good natural beach, and owed its existence as a port to a sun-trap location well sheltered from the wind. Even with the subsequent massive growth, the town maintains its separate identity and a refreshing sense of reality which is sometimes lacking at the newer resort next door. The focal point is the bustling harbour area, from where ferries depart for La Gomera.

PARQUE ECOLÓGICO AGUILAS DEL TEIDE ● ●
(EAGLES OF TEIDE ECOLOGICAL PARK)

Here's a lush, tropical park that kids will love as a change from the beach. Not just eagles, but condors, flamingos, pelicans and penguins number among the birdlife living here, while animals include crocodiles, pygmy hippos and tigers. If that's not enough to fill the day, the attractions on site include dodgem boats, a bobsleigh run and other rides.

PLAYA DE LAS AMÉRICAS ● ● ●

Love it or hate it, you should see it. Look out for the restaurant signs that boast, 'No Spanish food served here!' One of the most successful purpose-built resorts in the world, Playa de las Américas started construction at the end of the 1960s and has become almost a byword for how *not* to develop tourism. Unfocused, sprawling, much of it frankly ugly, and attracting low-budget packages, it nevertheless rightly remains supremely popular for a fun and sun holiday. Investment in its beaches has greatly improved the quality of the sand, the weather is perfect, and there's no doubt that for those who want to start the day with a full English breakfast at lunchtime, swim and tan all afternoon, and disco dance all night, this is the place.

28B1
Centro Cultural, Plaza del Carmen ☎ 922 757137
Hydrofoil and ferry services to La Gomera. Boat trips from the harbour

---

28B1
On Arona road, 3km from Los Cristianos
922 753001
Summer daily 9–6; winter 10–6
Few   Expensive
On site (££)
Free bus from resorts

28B1
Centro Comercial, near Parque Santiago II complex
☎ 922 797668
Boat excursions from Puerto Colón

Above: *a view from Puerto Colón, Costa Adeje*

75

An elegant balcony on a late 19th-century building in Adeje

What to See in the South

ADEJE ✪

One of the few places in the south with a natural water supply, this appealing, unspoiled little southern hilltown is the starting point for walks to the Barranco del Infierno (► 77). Though quite unremarkable now, it was once a Guanche tribal settlement and later became the Tenerife base of the counts of Gomera, who had plantations here worked by 1,000 African slaves. Ruins of the counts' fortress, Casa Fuerte, can be seen, and there's a 16th-century church, Iglesia de Santa Ursula.

COSTA DEL SILENCIO ✪

This resort at the island's southern tip was one of the first tourist developments, though its name has become rather incongruous since the construction here of Reina Sofía Airport. There are almost no proper beaches – just the odd shingle strip and a few coves – but several seawater swimming pools make up for the lack. Costa del Silencio includes Las Galletas, a former fishing hamlet with two small beaches and a waterfront promenade, and Ten-Bel, one of Tenerife's first purpose-built self-catering resorts.

> ### DID YOU KNOW?
>
> Ten-Bel, on the Costa del Silencio, takes its name from the nationalities of the two business partners who created it in 1969. One was from Tenerife, the other from Belgium.

EL MÉDANO ✪

A near-constant breeze has been both the blessing and the bane of Tenerife. El Médano, on the island's exposed southeast corner, has the best natural beaches, but is generally too windy for sunbathing to be enjoyable. There's a wind farm on the hills nearby, and this is the island's leading resort for windsurfing. International contests are held here, and anyone who really enjoys the sport should visit. The resort itself, on the headland of Punta del Médano, lacks charm and is very close to the international airport. Unspoiled pale beaches extend south to the hooknosed volcano at Punta Roja.

Barranco del Infierno

This excellent walk is much easier than the hike up Pico del Teide (► 69). It's on a good path with less weather problems and no risk of suffering from altitude sickness! The Barranco del Infierno itself (Hell Gorge) is the valley of a stream that rises on the southeastern slopes of the Teide National Park (over 2,000m above sea level). This walk covers the short stretch above Adeje, where the stream passes through a dramatic canyon, the deepest in the Canary Islands. Wear decent shoes (trainers will do in dry weather) and start as early in the day as possible to avoid crowds and the heat (carry water).

Distance
8km

Time
3–4 hours walking

Start/end point
Adeje
⊞ 28B2

Lunch
Otelo I (££)
✉ Adeje

Start at Adeje (► 76). Take the road that runs uphill through its centre. Continue on the steep road that leads to the gorge path.

The popular path through the Barranco del Infierno

At the entrance to the gorge, the path is fairly flat. Notice the caves high in the rock face – Guanche mummies were found in them. The rocky scenery is dramatic. The stream, at first contained in a concrete gulley, is the only permanent watercourse in the south. In places the vegetation is green and lush. Further on, the gorge becomes narrower.

The path crosses and re-crosses the stream, now no longer flowing through a gully.

There are some steep sections, but the total altitude gain is only 300m. Finally the path arrives at La Cascada, a waterfall in three levels pouring into a natural pool, where it is pleasant to rest and swim.

To return, there is no alternative but to follow the same path back.

+ 28C1
⊠ 3km from Exit 24 of
Autopista del Sur
🍴 Along Paseo Maritimo
(£–££)

+ 28B1
⊠ Exit 26 of Autopista del
Sur, 3km northeast of
Los Cristianos
☎ 922 795424
🕐 Daily 10–6
🍴 Restaurant on site (££)
🚌 Free shuttle bus from
Playa de las Américas
and Los Cristianos
♿ Few
Moderate
⬌ Costa del Silencio (➤ 76)

*Parques Exóticos, where
rainforest blooms flourish
in a tropical microclimate*

+ 28C2
⊠ On C821, 23km northeast
of Los Cristianos
🍴 El Sombrerito (££)
🚌 342 from Playa de las
Américas; 474 from
Granadilla; 482 from Los
Cristianos
⬌ Pico del Teide (➤ 18)

LOS ABRIGOS

A fishing village close to Reina Sofía Airport, Los Abrigos is noted for its first-rate waterfront fish restaurants and has two beaches. Behind the village the Golf del Sur development includes an excellent golf course.

PARQUES EXÓTICOS

An astonishing sight in the midst of so much barren terrain, this lush tropical garden east of Los Cristianos is truly exotic. The main attraction is Amazonia, a slice of tropical rainforest created inside a climatically controlled domed area; it's hot and muggy inside. Parrots, hummingbirds and 5,000 butterflies fly freely around.

Other attractions include a reptile house, a well-stocked cactus garden and a zoo park. Many of the animals are chosen with children in mind and include friendly marmosets and squirrel-monkeys. You can even go inside the cages.

VILAFLOR

Quite unlike other settlements in the south, the prettily named 'flower town' is the highest village in the Canary Islands. Standing at 1,160m, it rises through cultivated terraces to pine forest on the volcanic slopes of the Teide National Park. The vines of Vilaflor produce drinkable dry white wines, and the village also has an abundant natural spring whose waters are bottled and sold all over the island. Although millions pass through Vilaflor on their way to the national park, few pause here and it remains unspoiled. On the village outskirts are a couple of *artesanía* centres, useful places to buy local arts and crafts.

Just outside the village, set back from the main road, the little chapel called the Ermita de San Roque stands by the viewpoint Mirador de San Roque. From here there is a majestic panorama across southern Tenerife down to the dazzling coast.

A Drive in the South

Leave the resorts behind, climbing into near-barren sun-baked landscapes.

From Los Cristanos take the Arona road, C622 (changes to C822 after the Autopista junction).

Pass through the village of Valle de San Lorenzo to reach Mirador de la Centinela for a sweeping view over a landscape of volcanic cones.

About 2km further on, minor road 5114 turns left towards Vilaflor. It climbs steeply in places, eventually reaching the 5112 at Escalona, where you turn right to continue climbing. The road skirts Montaña del Pozo (1,294m).

Along here walled vineyard terraces climb the slopes to Vilaflor (▶ 78), the highest village in the Canary Islands, noted for its white wines.

On reaching Vilaflor, turn left onto the C821 and keep climbing.

Above the village, past the Ermita de San Roque, pause at the Mirador de San Roque for a tremendous view. Almost at once the road enters the fragrant pine forest that encircles Las Cañadas (▶ 68). A twisting mountain road through the forest gives more good *mirador* views as Pico del Teide comes into view.

The road leaves the forest and at Boca del Tauce enters the volcanic Caldera de las Cañadas (▶ 66). Take a left onto the C823 for Chío.

The road cuts across a dark landscape of cones and lava flows. Eventually you reach the pine forests once more. There's a pleasant picnic site and rest area (*zona recreativa*) near Chío. The road descends sharply. Before Chío there are good views down to the sea, with La Gomera visible across the water.

At the Chío junction turn left and left again onto the C822. Pass unspoiled little Guía de Isora. Cross a succession of barrancos (gorges), eventually reaching the Autopista del Sur. Take Exit 27 or 28 for Los Cristianos.

Distance
106km

Time
3 hours driving

Start/end point
Los Cristianos
✚ 28B1

Lunch stop
El Mirador (££)
✉ Mirador de San Roque, Vilaflor
Las Estrellas (££)
✉ Just before Chío

The drive passes through the pine forests of Los Retamares, above the village of Vilaflor

La Gomera

Despite efforts to attract visitors, the tiny island of La Gomera has so far escaped the onslaught of mass tourism. A wild green landscape of  plunging *barrancos* has made development difficult, just as it made colonisation impossible in centuries past. A new airport in the south may bring more people, but a lack of suitable facilities (though it does have two of the best hotels in the Canaries) ensures that La Gomera appeals mainly to those who need no entertaining, and want only to experience the simplicity and sun-warmed tranquillity of island life. Yet La Gomera offers walks, ancient woodland and a dramatic history. The island's capital, San Sebastián, is easily accessible by ferries crossing the 32km from southern Tenerife. Even for those who feel they must be back at their Tenerife hotel in time for dinner, La Gomera makes a most memorable day out.

'As we were passing, we observed an eruption of the volcano. The smoke and flames, the glowing masses of lava, the muffled roaring from the earth's interior, caused panic among the crew … They believed the volcano had erupted because we had undertaken this voyage.'

CHRISTOPHER COLUMBUS
Starting out from La Gomera on his first
voyage across the Atlantic (logbook, 1492)

●

The yellow-washed church at Vallehermoso

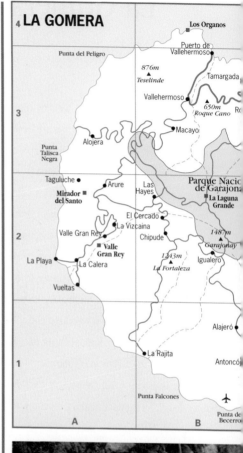

4 LA GOMERA

Los Organos

Puerto de Vallehermoso

Punta del Peligro

876m
Teselinde

Tamargada

Vallehermoso

650m
Roque Cano

Ro

3

Macayo

Punta Talisca Negra

Alojera

Taguluche ●

Arure

Las Hayes

Parque Nacio de Garajona

■ **La Laguna Grande**

Mirador ■ del Santo

El Cercado

La Vizcaina

Valle Gran Rey

Chipude

1487m
Garajonay

2

■ **Valle Gran Rey**

1343m
La Fortaleza

Igualero

La Playa ●

La Calera

Vueltas

Alajeró ●

1

La Rajita

Antoncó

Punta Falcones

Punta de Becerro

A

B

Punta
de Agulo

0   2   4   6 km

Agulo

Punta Gabiña

uego de
las Centro
Visitantes

Hermigua

Punta Majona

Cedro

Las
Poyatas

Valle de Hermigua

sque

del

arcita

Cedro

El Atajo

Ermita de NS
de Guadalupe

Punta
Llana

Degollada
de
Peraza

Parador de
San Sebastián
de La Gomera

oque
gando

Chigua

Vegaipala

663m
Roque del
Sombrero

SAN SEBASTIÁN
DE LA GOMERA

Tenerife

as
as

Punta Gorda

Playa de
Santiago

Punta Gaviota

C

D

Below: *La Playa, a shingle
beach near Valle Gran
Rey*

Left: *a goatherd moves
her flock along a
mountain road*

✚ 83C3
✉ 27km from San Sebastián
on the northern road
🍴 Las Rosas (££) in Las
Rosas hamlet, 2km west
↔ Hermigua (► 85)
❓ Fiesta of San Marcos 25
Apr; Los Piques mid–late
Jun (silbo language)

✚ 82B2
✉ 29km west from San
Sebastián, off the central
highland routes
🍴 Village bars (£)
↔ Parque Nacional de
Garajonay (► 26)

Above: the view of Pico
del Teide from Agulo

AGULO ★★

A pearl of a village in a delightful setting above the coast,
Agulo is enclosed by a semicircle of steep green hills,
pouring with waterfalls and streams after rain showers.
The town's narrow cobbled streets are focused on a
domed Moorish-looking church, while out to sea the
inspiring vision of Pico del Teide rises above the clouds
from the dark floating form that is Tenerife. It's one of the
prettiest spots on the north coast.

CHIPUDE ★★

Until recently Chipude was a remote hamlet, lost high in
the green heart of the island. Among Gomerans its name
used to be synonymous with a rustic way of life and
poverty, and locals say that the people of Chipude used to
drive away intruders with stones.

While better roads and communications have changed
all that, the villagers thankfully still preserve their old
customs and traditions, and it is here that you may hear
silbo – not being demonstrated for tourists, but used to call
to friends or neighbours (► 99).

Chipude has long been noted for its handmade pots
made without a potter's wheel and decorated with traditional Guanche motifs, though in fact these are more often
from the neighbouring village of El Cercado. In the
surrounding area are other small, barely accessible rustic
villages, including Pavón and Temocodá, also known for
their fine handmade pots.

Legend has it that the extraordinary rock formation
known as La Fortaleza, or the Chipude Fort, 2km south of
the village, was a Guanche sacred site. This is easy to
believe – its sheer stone soars vertically more than 1,200m
to a tabletop crest.

HERMIGUA

Lying in the island's most fertile and productive valley, Hermigua tacks along the road through plantations of banana palms. Though one of La Gomera's larger settlements, it's a tiny, tranquil place, a stopping point for visitors who want to see local crafts being made and maybe make a purchase at the interesting Los Telares *artesanía* (craft centre). Nearly opposite is the Convento de Santo Domingo, a 16th-century church with a Moorish-style wooden ceiling.

LOS ÓRGANOS (THE ORGANS)

Inaccessible from the land, these strange slender columns of basalt emerging from the sea to the northwest of Puerto de Vallehermoso are so named because they resemble organ pipes.

Extending over a 200m stretch of cliff, and rising as much as 80m from the sea, the tightly packed hexagonal columns make an impressive sight, and they certainly provide a good excuse for a boat excursion (see side panel for pick-up points). Surprisingly, they do look just like the pipes of some gigantesque organ.

PARQUE NACIONAL DE GARAJONAY (➤ 26, TOP TEN)

PLAYA DE SANTIAGO

This southerly point of the island is the site of one of La Gomera's most ambitious tourist projects. High on the cliffs above the stony beach stands the delightful Hotel Jardín Tecina, owned by the ferry operator Fred Olsen. Scattered over its huge and beautiful grounds are separate accommodation units (described as 'superior duplex bungalows'). Its impressive facilities include several restaurants and a beach club reached by a cliff lift. Below the hotel, the former fishing village is steadily expanding with bars and restaurants.

At one end, a small fisherman's chapel decorated with model boats is set into the rock-face. La Gomera's new airport lies nearby.

Craft production at Los Telares, Hermigua

83C3
- 20km from San Sebastián on the northern road
- El Silbo (£), a simple bar-restaurant in the village
- Agulo (➤ 84)

82B4
- 52km from San Sebastián on north coast
- Bars in Vallehermoso (£),
- Only accessible by boat, either from Puerto de Vallehermoso (4km from Los Órganos), or on longer excursions from Playa de Santiago, Vueltas or San Sebastián
- Vallehermoso (➤ 88)

83C1
- 30km southwest from San Sebastián
- Edificio Las Vistas, Local 8, Avenida Marítima s/n
- ☎ 922 895650
- Simple bars and restaurants on the waterfront (£–££), Hotel Jardín Tecina (££–£££)
- Parque Nacional de Garajonay (➤ 26)

83D2

On the east coast of island

Calle Real 4
☎ 922 141512

Bars in town (£); good food at the Parador de San Sebastián de la Gomera (£££)

The intermittent bus service is not reliable. Taxis are readily available at the ferry dock

Parque Nacional de Garajonay (➤ 26)

Fiestas include the local saint's festival around 20 Jan; Carnaval (Carnival) about the end of Feb; Semana Colombina (Columbus Week) 1–6 Sep; Virgen de Guadaloupe 1–6 Oct

Pozo de la Aguada

Calle Real
☎ 922 141512
Mon–Sat 9–1:30, 3:30–6, Sun 10–1
None
Free
In the same building as the tourist office

Iglesia Nuestra Señora de la Asunción

Calle Real
None
Free

Casa de Colón

Calle Real 56
☎ 922 870155
Mon–Fri 9–1, 4:30–7:30, Sat 9–1
None
Free

SAN SEBASTIÁN DE LA GOMERA

La Gomera's capital, usually known as San Sebastián and often known to locals simply as Villa, is an unprepossessing little port, though it has an excellent harbour. In several ways San Sebastián is quite untypical of the island. Though hemmed in by hills, the town lies on flat ground while the rest of La Gomera is all steep slopes and valleys; its dusty, dry setting is a marked contrast to the island's exotic greenery. Most of the town is modern white cubes in an island full of rustic character. Only San Sebastián's picturesque main street, Calle Real (sometimes known as Calle del Medio), and the main square, Plaza de las Américas, with its balconied mansions, evoke the memory of colonial times and the great drama of the island's history.

La Gomera was the last Canary Island to be subjugated by the Spanish – it remained independent until 1837. As a result, no other Canary Island retains so much of the native Guanche culture and ethnicity. There are, too, visible in many island faces, reminders of the many African slaves who were kept here.

When Christopher Columbus anchored at San Sebastián before the voyage that discovered the Americas, this was the most westerly port in the world. Tenerife remained in Guanche hands, while on La Gomera only this edge of the island was under Spanish control.

To recapture a little of that past, walk along the main street, Calle Real. Here is the 17th-century Casa del Pozo, once the customs house; the name means House of the Well. Inside is the **Pozo de la Aguada**, the well from which Columbus's quartermaster drew the water to supply his ships on the outward voyage to America. Here too the expedition bought seeds, grains and flowers to be planted in the New World.

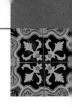

In the same street stands the **Iglesia Nuestra Señora de la Asunción** (Church of Our Lady of the Assumption), where – we are told, but this is poetic licence – Columbus said his last prayer before setting out on the great voyage. Founded in the 15th-century, the church was largely rebuilt in the late 18th century.

Also in Calle Real, **Casa de Colón** (Columbus House) has no proven link with the explorer, but is now claimed as the house where he lodged. It has been restored as a museum about Columbus, featuring models of his ships and old maps, and is the focal point of the town's annual week-long Columbus festival in September.

Finally, in the harbourside park, the **Torre del Conde** (Count's Tower, closed to visitors) is the oldest building in continuous use in the Canary Islands. This sturdy tower house dates from 1447, and was once the residence of Beatriz de Bobadilla (▶ 14), wife of the count of La Gomera, Hernán Peraza (whose father had built the tower). Both the count and the countess were hated by the Guanches for their repressive arrogance and cruelty. Hernán was eventually murdered for raping (or seducing) a Guanche princess, and Beatriz moved into this tower for her own protection.

The tower also has a connection with Columbus: after the murder of the count, Columbus became friendly with the Beatriz. Later the tower became a storehouse for gold, silver and treasures looted from Native Americans and sent back to Spain.

Iglesia Nuestra Señora de la Asunción
✉ Calle Real
♿ None
🎫 Free

Casa de Colón
✉ Calle Real 56
☎ 922 870155
🕐 Mon–Fri 9–1, 4:30–7:30, Sat 9–1
♿ None
🎫 Free

Opposite: *the Torre del Conde, built by Hernán Peraza the Elder*
Below: *the harbour at San Sebastián*

🕂 82A2

✉ 44km from San Sebastián

ℹ Calle Lepanto, La Playa, Valle Gran Rey ☎ 922 805458

🍽 Bars and fish restaurants on the coast, or the César Manrique *mirador* restaurant (£–££)

🚌 Occasional buses and boats from San Sebastián

❓ Los Santos Reyes fiesta 6 Jan (Epiphany)

Above: *La Playa is perhaps the best beach on the island*

VALLE GRAN REY ✪✪✪

On the west side of the island, the majestic Valley of the Great King is still remote and was almost unknown until the 1970s. Then it was a retreat for various Greens and hippies – offering an away-from-it-all, ecologically sustainable lifestyle. Today, though, and despite the location, it attracts more visitors than anywhere else on the island.

On the twisting road up to Arure (10km inland), several viewpoints offer stunning panoramas of cultivated terraces clinging to the lower slopes of the steep ravine, the scattered white houses of a few hamlets, and the valley opening out to greenery beside the vibrant blue sea. One hamlet has a spectacularly located *mirador* restaurant designed by Lanzarote architect César Manrique.

The road descends the ravine to reach La Calera, the attractive little central community of the Valle Gran Rey, standing among banana plantations. Beyond, the road divides for the last 1km to the sea: to the to the north is La Playa; to the south is the fishing harbour and port at Vueltas, the traditional gateway to the valley. Both settlements have simple waterside eateries offering the freshest of fish. La Playa and Vueltas have developed as tourist centres since the 1980s and their little shingle beaches are among the best that La Gomera offers.

🕂 82B3

✉ 48km northwest of San Sebastián

🍽 Bar-restaurants in the village centre (£)

↔ Los Órganos (► 85)

VALLEHERMOSO ✪✪✪

An attractive and appealing village – one of the island's largest communities – Vallehermoso is indeed in a 'beautiful valley' as its name suggests. It is surrounded by forest, vineyards and palm plantations of date and banana. A striking 650m-high volcanic pinnacle close by is called Roque Cano, Dog Rock, supposedly for its resemblance to a canine tooth.

Northern Gomera

The deeply cut, forested terrain of La Gomera restricts access, and until recently most journeys were made by boat, around the coastline of the island.

Start out from San Sebastián on the Hermigua road, TF711.

The road climbs steeply up the Barranco del Cedro, giving views over the water to Tenerife, and passes by a large statue of Christ that overlooks San Sebastián.

The road climbs higher and skirts the edges of the Parque Nacional de Garajonay.

Here the road winds through unspoiled mixed woodland of laurel, beech, pine and flowering heather trees, despite the particular name for this area, Bosque del Cedro (Cedar Forest).

After sharp turns and a tunnel, the road begins descending towards the north coast.

Wonderful views contrast green valleys and the blue ocean as the road descends into Hermigua (► 85) and, 3km further, Agulo (► 84).

The road, winding all the time, climbs inland beside a plunging green valley, passing Las Rosas restaurant and continuing to Vallehermoso.

At Tamargada, pause at a fine *mirador* to look at the forest. At Vallehermoso (► 88) there is abundant cultivation of date palms and bananas. Many palm trees have been cut and have metal cups attached to gather the sap for La Gomera's speciality, *miel de palma*, a syrup made from sugar palm sap.

A poor road leads down to the shore at Puerto de Vallehermoso.

From the harbour, regular boat trips go out to see the strange rock formations of Los Órganos (► 85).

Distance
50km

Time
2–3 hours

Start point
San Sebastián de la Gomera
✚ 83D2

End point
Puerto de Vallehermoso
✚ 82B4

Lunch
Restaurant Las Rosas (££), or Tambur bar-restaurant (£) at the Juego de Bolas Visitor Centre

A narrow green valley beyond Vallehermoso

Where To...

Above: *souvenir brooches on a pavement stall*
Right: *a shop sign in La Laguna*
Left: *Playa Jardín, Puerto de la Cruz*

The North

Prices
Approximate price of a three-course meal for one, without drinks:

£ = under €18
££ = €18–36
£££ = over €36

Norwegian Connection
The ethnographic park containing the Pyramids of Güímar, on the east coast of Tenerife, first proposed by Norwegian explorer and anthropologist Thor Heyerdahl, has been funded by shipping magnate Fred Olsen, a fellow Norwegian (▶ 44). There's more about the Tenerife pyramids on the FERCO website, www.ferco.org.

Bajamar
Café Melita (£)
More of a café and cake shop than a restaurant, this German-run place in the little north coast resort specialises in desserts, pastries and rich cakes. Lovely sea views.
✉ Carretera General ☎ 922 540814 🕓 Daily 10–5 🚌 105 (Santa Cruz–Punta Hidalgo) half-hourly

Candelaria
El Arquete (££)
There's high-quality creative Canarian cooking at this smarter than usual restaurant, something of a find in this part of the island. It makes a pleasant lunch spot after seeing the church in the little pilgrimage town.
✉ Lomo de Aroba 2 ☎ 922 500115 🕓 Mon–Sat lunch

El Sauzal
Casa del Vino (££)
The interesting wine museum and wine-tasting centre in El Sauzal also has a good, lively restaurant, which for some is the main reason to visit. The outdoor terrace has sea views.
✉ La Baranda ☎ 922 563886 🕓 Tue–Sat 1–4, 8–midnight, Sun lunch

La Ermita (££)
Accomplished seafood and international dishes attract a varied clientele to this quietly set restaurant on the outskirts of town. Local wines are available from the cask. The dining room is smart but relaxing, decorated with plants and ceramics.
✉ Urb. Los Angeles ☎ 922 575380 🕓 Mon–Tue, Thu–Sat lunch, dinner, Sun lunch

La Laguna
Casa Maquila (££)
La Laguna is not a place for fine dining, though there are some good restaurants out of town. While sightseeing in the centre, choose a typical tapas bar and settle down to local specialities, properly prepared – at somewhere like this simple and agreeable restaurant.
✉ Callejón de Maquila 4 ☎ 922 257020 🕓 Lunch, dinner

Hoya del Camello (££)
It's a short distance out of town, but this moderately priced establishment is one of the La Laguna area's better restaurants, with a good range of well-prepared international, Spanish and Canarian favourites.
✉ Carretera General del Norte 128, San Lazaro ☎ 922 262054 🕓 Lunch, dinner. Closed early May, late Aug, Sun eve

Los Naranjeros
Los Limoneros (£££)
This rural but very civilised spot off the motorway near La Laguna draws local families for big, well-prepared dinners and weekend feasts of international and local specialities, including rabbit in spicy sauce, and lamb and goat dishes. Service is good.
✉ Carreterra General del Norte, Los Naranjeros, 4km east of Tacoronte ☎ 922 636637 🕓 Mon–Sat 12–midnight

San Andrés
The cluster of humble restaurants (£–££) along the waterfront of this little harbour village is well known to locals. They all serve

seafood and the fresh catch of the day, at similar prices. Just beyond is Playa de las Teresitas, the island's most beautiful beach.

Ramón (££)

Like its neighbours, Ramón specialises in seafood, and is one of the most reputable of the restaurants behind the glorious Playa de Las Teresitas. Decor is simple, light and bright with green and white tiles festooned with plants.

✉ Calle Dique 23 ☎ 922 549308 🕓 Daily 11AM–11PM

Santa Cruz

Café del Príncipe (£–££)

Attractive and authentic place, well situated in one of the most appealing squares in Santa Cruz. Sit out with locals and tourists and enjoy a drink, a snack or a complete meal of typical island specialities.

✉ Plaza del Príncipe de Asturias ☎ 922 278810 🕓 Tue–Sun 9–midnight

El Coto de Antonio (££)

Rambla del General Franco curves round the city centre. Along here, and northwest of the road, there are several smart eating places catering mainly for business people and well-to-do locals but also tourists. This is a top example, serving good fresh cooking from seasonal ingredients.

✉ Calle General Goded 13 ☎ 922 272105 🕓 Mon–Fri lunch, dinner, Sat dinner. Closed 1–15 Aug

Los Troncos (££)

Among the very best restaurants in the Tenerife capital, in the smart northwest area, and yet surprisingly inexpensive. Noted for Canarian cooking of a high standard, and also for Basque specialities.

✉ Calle General Goded 17

☎ 922 284152 🕓 Thu–Tue. Closed Sun dinner & mid-Aug to mid-Sep

Olympo (£)

This popular bar-restaurant may be touristy, but locals also gather here to enjoy a drink or a meal in a pleasant setting in the heart of town. Good set lunch at a moderate price.

✉ Plaza de la Candelaria ☎ 922 241738 🕓 10AM–midnight

Parque Marítimo César Manrique (£–£££)

It was part of César Manrique's philosophy that all tourist attractions should offer good eating and drinking facilities on site. The lido on the Santa Cruz waterfront does visitors proud, with a range of eating places from a café to more formal restaurants.

✉ Avenida de la Constitución ☎ 922 202995 🕓 Daily 10–6

Tegueste

Casa Tomás (£)

A simple, family-run restaurant west of La Laguna (by the church in El Portezuelo). Cooking is homely and authentic, and the wines are local, sometimes straight from the cask. *Costillas con papas* (cutlets with potatoes) is a typical dish.

✉ El Portezuelo ☎ 922 250547 🕓 Sep–Jul, Tue–Sun 12am–11pm

El Drago (£££)

One of Tenerife's leading restaurants, this charming old farmhouse near Tegueste produces classic Canarian cooking; specialities include local cheeses, fish casseroles and rabbit in spicy sauce.

✉ Calle Marqués de Celada 2, El Socorro ☎ 922 543001 🕓 Tue–Sun lunch, Fri–Sat dinner. Closed Aug

Anaga Views

Most accessible of the Anaga viewpoints is Mirador de Jardina, near La Laguna. Much higher is Mirador Cruz del Carmen (920m), which gives a view of both coasts. Here stands a lonely 17th-century chapel, the Ermita Cruz del Carmen. Alongside there is a restaurant, and an information centre on the Parque Rural de Anaga (► 48). A short distance further along the road, on the slope of Taborno, Mirador Pico del Inglés (992m) is the highest viewpoint. Nearer the northern tip of the range, Mirador del Bailadero (759m) gives a lofty view onto the village of Taganana.

The West

Canary Wine

'But that which most takes my Muse and me,
Is a pure cup of Canary Wine.'

Ben Jonson, *Epigrammes: Inviting a Friend to Supper* (1616)

Canaries – Islands, Birds and Dogs

It is sometimes thought that the Canaries are named after the canary, a yellow cage bird seen all over the world. The bird is a Canary Islands native, and common in western Tenerife – although the wild native has a less brilliant plumage than the cage variety. However, the bird is named after the islands rather than the other way round. The Canary Islands were so named for the wild dogs (Latin *canis, canes*) that had been observed by early visitors on the island of Fuerteventura.

Buenavista del Norte
La Cabaña (£)

Good-value home cooking attracts both visitors and locals to this simple place in Tenerife's most westerly town. Fresh fish is a staple on the menu.

✉ Calle El Puerto 26 ☎ 922 127050 🕓 Thu–Tue lunch, dinner

Garachico
Isla Baja (££)

Respected due to its long-standing reputation, this rather pricey restaurant is located on the waterfront facing the Castillo de San Miguel. It specialises in good local fish dishes, though you can also stop for just a drink, snack or ice cream.

✉ Calle Esteban de Ponte 5 ☎ 922 830008 🕓 Lunch, dinner 🚌 363 (Puerto–Buenavista) hourly

Icod de los Vinos
Carmen (££)

Considered the best place to relax, get away from the coach parties and tuck in to some traditional Spanish cooking before or after peering at the giant Dragon Tree nearby.

✉ Avenida de Las Canarias 1 ☎ 922 810631 🕓 Lunch, dinner 🚌 354, 363 (Puerto–Icod) both hourly

La Orotava
Sabor Canario (££)

Set in a fine, late 16th-century building, this charming restaurant is attached to the Museo del Pueblo Guanche in the heart of the old town – a showcase for Canarian crafts and food products. It serves authentic local dishes – try braised rabbit, roast cheeses or *ropa vieja* (literally 'old clothes', a classic Canarian hotpot). Head for a table in the plant-filled courtyard.

✉ Calle Carrera 17 ☎ 922 323725 🕓 Mon–Sat lunch, dinner

Los Gigantes/Puerto de Santiago
Casa Pancho (££)

This authentic restaurant comes as a surprise in a popular sun-and-sea resort area, catering mainly to British people on package holidays and with few signs of any indigenous local life. A genuine Spanish restaurant serving Spanish food to a high standard – there's nowhere else quite as good for some distance.

✉ Playa de la Arena ☎ 922 101323 🕓 Jul–May, Tue–Sat lunch, dinner 🚌 473 (Los Gigantes–Las Galletas, south of Los Cristianos)

Miranda (££)

Imaginative local and international cuisine in the heart of Los Gigantes. Light, modern decor and a good range of steaks, seafood and Canarian wines.

✉ Calle Flor de Pascua 25 ☎ 922 860207 🕓 Dinner

Tamara (££)

Grandstand views over the resort and its giant cliffs give this restaurant much of its appeal. The ambience is relaxed and quiet.

✉ Avenida Maritima, Los Gigantes ☎ 922 860011 🕓 Lunch, dinner

Masca
Chez Arlette/Casa Enrique (£)

The attractive location on the main road by the church

makes this place a local favourite. From its rustic bamboo-shaded terrace decked with simple wooden furnishings stretch magnificent vistas of the gorge below. The menu runs to things like maize cake and grilled lamb, washed down with home-made lemonade or local wines.

✉ La Piedra ☎ 922 863459
🕓 Sun–Fri 11.30AM–6.30PM

Parque Nacional del Teide (Teide National Park)
(*including boundary area*)
El Mesón del Teide (££)

On the Puerto de la Cruz side of the national park, this attractive place pulls in the crowds at lunchtime for wholesome Canarian fare on the steep climb above La Oratava.

✉ Carretera General 821
☎ 922 354801 🕓 Lunch

Restaurante Las Estrellas (££)

Out of the crossroads village of Chío, on the southwest side of the national park boundary, this bar-restaurant enjoys stirring views over the coasts.

✉ Chío 🕓 All day 🚌 460 (Icod–Guía de Isora, via Chío) every 2–3 hours

Parador las Cañadas del Teide (££)

This spectacular *parador* is close to Pico del Teide and all the major volcanic sites. The restaurant is unpretentious but correct, offers good food and is open to the public.

✉ Parque Nacional del Teide
☎ 922 386415 🕓 Lunch, dinner 🚌 343 (Playa de las Américas–Las Cañadas) once

daily meets 348 (Puerto–Las Cañadas) once daily

Puerto de la Cruz
Casa de Miranda (££)

This traditional Canarian house near Puerto's harbour square traces its ancestry back to 1730. A cheerful *tapas* bar decked with gingham tablecloths, red chilli peppers and hams occupies the ground floor; upstairs its galleried, plant-filled restaurant makes a romantic setting for Canarian and international fare at reasonable prices.

✉ Plaza de Europa ☎ 922 373871 🕓 Lunch, dinner

Casino Taoro (£££)

Puerto's casino is in Parque Taoro, the park set back from and above the bustle of the town. The casino restaurant attracts a dressed-up crowd and caters for them in style, with red-draped tables, formal service, smart atmosphere and a predictable range of classy international dishes. Good views.

✉ Casino, Parque Taoro
☎ 922 380550 🕓 Dinner

La Papaya (££)

Enter this 200-year-old house in the historic quarter and ramble through a series of plant-filled dining rooms and Andalucian-style garden patios; the ambience is utterly captivating. It's a peaceful place, though a caged bird or two may squawk an occasional remark. Seafood and rabbit feature on the menu, and the service is friendly.

✉ Calle del Lomo 10
☎ 922 382811 🕓 Thu–Tue 12:30–11:30PM

African Wind

Claims that Tenerife's climate is 'perpetual spring' are belied by periods of sirocco. This hot, dry, dusty wind blows straight off the Sahara desert for days at a time, usually in spring and autumn. Temperatures rise to as much as 45°C. Sirocco spells are known to locals as *el tiempo de África* (African weather).

95

Be Polite

You'll notice that locals entering or leaving a restaurant often address the room at large with a quiet greeting of *'Señores, señoras'*. This is simple politeness. When speaking to Spaniards, a formal use of titles is considered normal and makes a good impression even if your Spanish is not very good. Address men as *Señor*, women as *Señora*, and young unmarried women as *Señorita*.

La Parilla (£££)

This smart restaurant is located in one of Tenerife's most luxurious hotels, the Botánico, but is open to the public. It offers top international and French-style cooking, and slick service in an elegant setting. Dress is smart-casual.

✉ **Hotel Botánico, Avenida Richard J Yeoward** ☎ **922 311400** ◷ **Dinner**

Lago Martiánez (£–£££)

Several quality bars and restaurants provide snacks, drinks and complete meals in this attractive lake and pool complex (► 60).

✉ **Playa Martiánez** ☎ **922 383852** ◷ **Daily 10–5, then Andromeda open in evenings until late**

Magnolia (£££)

Top-class dining, indoors or alfresco, at this award-winning restaurant attracts discerning locals and well-to-do Spanish visitors. Food is a mix of Catalan and international, with an emphasis on fish and seafood. You'll find the restaurant out of town in the La Paz *urbanización*.

✉ **Carretera del Botánico 5, Avenida del Marqués de Villanueva del Prado** ☎ **922 385614** ◷ **Dinner**

Mi Vaca y Yo (££)

It looks down to earth and rustic, but this restaurant near the old fishing harbour is one of the best in town for exceptional fish and seafood dishes. There are lots of traditional Canarian dishes on the menu, but also Spanish and international favourites.

✉ **Calle Cruz Verde 3** ☎ **922 385247** ◷ **Dinner**

Palatino (££)

An excellent range of seafood in a long-established and well-regarded restaurant near the old fishing harbour. An elegant setting near the Plaza del Charco.

✉ **Calle del Lomo 28** ☎ **922 382374** ◷ **Mon–Sat lunch, dinner. Closed Jul**

Rancho Grande (£)

This bustling waterfront café near the San Telmo chapel is an attractive and convenient location for a quick snack. Cakes, drinks, snacks and inexpensive meals are available all day into the evening, to eat in or take away. The shop alongside stocks plenty of attractive goodies to buy as presents.

✉ **Calle San Telmo 10** ☎ **922 383752** ◷ **Daily from 10AM**

Régulo (££)

Popular, atmospheric and attractive with its plants and patio, this is an agreeable example of the many good little fish restaurants near the old fishing harbour, in the quarter near Plaza del Charco.

✉ **Calle San Felipe 16** ☎ **922 384506** ◷ **Mon–Sat lunch, dinner. Closed Jul**

Santa Ursula
Los Corales (££)

In the Santa Ursula area, about 10km north of Puerto, several good little restaurants like this specialise in typical Canarian fish stews, and fried eel, as well as a range of more familiar dishes. Local wines accompany the food.

✉ **Cuesta de la Villa 30** ☎ **922 302261** ◷ **Tue–Sat lunch, dinner**

The South &
La Gomera

Adeje
Otelo I (££)
Get a drink or a good meal at this modest, likeable bar-restaurant, brilliantly situated near the entrance to the Barranco del Infierno. Well known to expatriates and old Tenerife hands, it's especially popular for the island's traditional rabbit dishes, spicy chicken and Canarian specialities. Hearty portions and a pleasant atmosphere.

✉ Calle Los Molinos, Barranco del Infierno ☎ 922 780374 🕐 Wed–Mon 10AM–midnight

El Médano
Avencio (£)
This reliable, inexpensive seafront favourite offers a cosy interior of rustic and nautical decor. Fresh seafood is always a safe bet, but there's plenty else on the menu. Catalan and Rioja wines accompany local vintages.

✉ Calle Chasna 6 ☎ 922 176079 🕐 Oct–Aug, Tue–Sun. Closed Sun dinner

Los Abrigos
La Langostera (£–££)
Drive past Golf del Sur developments and down to the sea. This is just one of a cluster of tempting little fish restaurants at this tiny waterside harbour along the Costa del Silencio. Here the fish is sold by weight: enjoy the freshest and simplest of Canarian cooking, with some good inexpensive wine.

✉ Paseo Maritimo ☎ 922 170302 🕐 Lunch, dinner

Perlas del Mar (££)
Of all the fish restaurants lining the water's edge at Los Abrigos, this one has perhaps the best location, just above the waterline. Select your fish from the counter and specify how you want it cooked (steamed, grilled, fried). Terrace tables make a fine spot to watch the sun set over the waves and the planes landing and taking off from Reina Sofía Airport.

✉ Paseo Maritimo ☎ 922 170014 🕐 Lunch, dinner

Los Cristianos
The resort has scores of tourist-oriented eating places, with more of them reaching a high standard of service and cuisine than is the case in neighbouring Playa de las Américas.

Casa del Mar (££)
On a corner of the busy Los Cristianos harbour, this upstairs restaurant offers a good view over the port, and serves a choice of Canarian, Spanish and international favourites.

✉ Esplanada del Muelle ☎ 922 793275 🕐 Tue–Sun lunch, dinner

Don Armando (£)
This Spanish-looking place adds a welcome touch of regional authenticity. Beyond the typically darkish bar (where plenty of Spanish voices can be heard) a light and spacious terrace restaurant has a grandstand view of the seafront. The all-day menu suggests classic *tapas* like grilled sardines, steamed mussels or potato croquettes, all at moderate prices.

✉ Calle San Telmo ☎ 922 796145 🕐 Daily from lunchtime

Trade Winds
On Tenerife and La Gomera the northerly trade winds – known as *los alisios* – bring settled weather of rainfree days with some cloud. On the north or west of the islands, the winds can be troublesome, and cloud cover excessive. In the south, it means perfect holiday weather.

Ethnic Restaurants

If you'd rather eat good-quality Italian food than search out Spanish in the heart of the big resorts, life will be easy. The Little Italy chain has nine good restaurants in Playa de las Américas and Los Cristianos – all with Little Italy in their name. If you prefer Chinese, look out for branches of Slow Boat (several in the main southern resorts).

Las Gangarras (££)

This attractive restaurant stands in one of the dry ravines behind the resort, amid typically rustic Canarian surroundings. The cooking is classic country style, using some organic produce.

📧 **Barranco Oscuro, Buzanada** ☎ **922 766423** 🕐 **Tue–Sat lunch, dinner**

Papa Luigi (£–££)

A cosy Italian restaurant in the town centre, cheerfully decorated with terracotta pots and gingham cloths. The menu presents an extensive range of familiar variations on the themes of pasta and pizza, in addition to a selection of fish and meat dishes. Cooking is more than competent and the service is courteously efficient.

📧 **Avenida Suecia 40** ☎ **922 750911** 🕐 **Lunch, dinner**

Playa de las Américas/Costa Adeje

There are literally hundreds of almost identical restaurants along the coast road through the resort. Their basic meals of pasta, pizza, paella, steak or fish and chips, and other international favourites are displayed in photos on boards outside.

El Molino Blanco (££)

A white windmill marks the spot, on the inland side of the resort. Though geared mainly towards foreign tourists, the rustic setting and welcoming atmosphere promise an enjoyable visit. Dining areas spill on to shady flower-filled terraces. Both wine list and menu are wide-ranging, with unusual items like goat or ostrich.

📧 **Avenida de Austria 5, San Eugenio Alto** ☎ **922 796282** 🕐 **Wed–Mon 1PM–1AM**

El Patio (£££)

Among the very best dining experiences on the south coast. Enjoy a high-quality Canarian and Spanish meal on the terrace of this hotel-restaurant near the Puerto Colón, where Playa de las Américas meets Costa Adeje.

📧 **Jardín Tropical Hotel, Calle Gran Bretaña, Urbanización San Eugenio** ☎ **922 750100** 🕐 **Dinner**

La Hacienda (£££)

One of the elegant restaurants in the luxury hotel complex of the Bahía del Duque. Dress up for a memorable treat.

📧 **Gran Hotel Bahía del Duque, Playa del Duque** ☎ **922 746900** 🕐 **Lunch, dinner**

Mamma Rosa (£££)

This very popular restaurant demands a certain smartness from diners to match the good food, fine wine and professional service. Despite the name, the food is not exclusively Italian.

📧 **Apartamentos Colón II, Los Moritos** ☎ **922 797823** 🕐 **Lunch, dinner**

Poris de Abona

Casablanca (££)

Leave the motorway at the Porís exit to track down this spacious pastel-toned restaurant near the seafront. Cuisine includes paella and home-made cheese. Look out for the interesting house wine, Viña Chajaña. Live folk music is an additional draw.

📧 **Carretera General** ☎ **922 164296** 🕐 **Tue–Sun lunch, dinner**

San Isidro

El Jable (££)

In this untouristy inland village near the motorway, close to the El Médano exit, there's an appealing and popular bar-restaurant serving hearty Canarian cooking.

✉ Calle Bentejui 9 ☎ 922 390698 🕐 Mon–Sat 1–4, 7:30–11. Closed Mon lunch 🚌 111 (Playa de las Américas–Santa Cruz)

Vilaflor

El Mirador (£–££)

The name tells you everything – this restaurant-bar stands just off the road below Mirador de San Roque, by the little Ermitage de San Roque. Enjoy outstanding views and good Canarian cooking.

✉ On C821, Ermita de San Roque ☎ 922 709135 🕐 Lunch 🚌 342 daily from Playa de las Américas; 482 from Los Cristianos; 474 from Granadilla

El Sombrerito (£–££)

The village restaurant of El Sombrerito belongs to Casa Chicho, the family-run inn. In Chicho and Ana's simple, friendly restaurant you can enjoy authentic Tenerife country recipes. There's a little farm museum and shop attached.

✉ Calle Santa Catalina ☎ 922 709052 🕐 Lunch, dinner 🚌 342 daily from Playa de las Américas; 482 from Los Cristianos; 474 from Granadilla

La Gomera

Casa del Mar (£–££)

This light, airy bar-restaurant near the seafront has a large menu of seafood and carefully prepared dishes, attracting local as well as tourist custom. Try the fish stew (*cazuela*). Lighter snacks are also available.

✉ Avenida Fred Olsen 2, San Sebastián ☎ 922 871219 🕐 Mon–Sat lunch, dinner

Hotel Jardín Tecina Restaurant (££)

The terrace of this excellent hotel on La Gomera's south coast offers international dining and a wonderful view of the sea.

✉ Lomada de Tecina, Playa de Santiago ☎ 922 145850 🕐 Lunch, dinner

Las Rosas (££)

Not just a place to eat, this pretty roadside restaurant is an essential stopover on a tour of La Gomera. Its superb valley-edge location and views and, most of all, its fascinating demonstrations of *el silbo* (see panel, right), the island's unique whistling language, attract coach parties every day. However, the Canarian specialities are delightful too.

✉ Las Rosas ☎ 922 800916 🕐 Lunch

El Silbo (£)

This modest bar-restaurant stands on the main road just north of the village. Its flower-decked terrace is a charming spot to enjoy an inexpensive drink or meal with a view.

✉ Hermigua ☎ 922 880304 🕐 Tue–Sun lunch, dinner

Parador de San Sebastián de la Gomera (££–£££)

This *parador* (➤ 105) has the best food on the island; Spanish and international cuisine.

✉ Llano de la Horca 1 ☎ 922 871100 🕐 Lunch, dinner

El Silbo

Of all the distinctive elements in Canarian culture, few are more astonishing than the 'whistling language' of La Gomera. In response to similar conditions that gave rise to yodelling in Switzerland – needing to communicate across steep terrain and dense forests – the Gomerans developed a whole vocabulary, syntax and grammar of whistles. Another quality of *el silbo* is its volume: skilled *silbadores* can whistle a detailed message to another person several kilometres away (➤ 84).

The North

Prices

For a double room in mid-season expect to pay:

£ = under €72
££ = €72–120
£££ = over €120

Timeshare Dreams

Tenerife is timeshare land, where touts pester, lure and tempt the unwary into signing away their savings in exchange for a week-a-year at a resort apartment block. Lavish inducements are given, not just to sign, but even to see the property. Timeshare is not a bad idea in principle – you don't have to use your annual week or two weeks; you can rent them out, or swap them for a fortnight in Florida or Florence. Don't agree to pay anything without legal advice and be sure you are informed about Spanish property law and taxes.

Güimar

Finca Salamanca (££)

This charming farmhouse in lush gardens makes a delightful stay. Avocado, mango and citrus groves surround the hotel and the building's rustic architecture makes a perfect backdrop for stylish decor and Hispanic arts and crafts. A barn contains an airy raftered restaurant serving Canarian specialities and local wines.

✉ **Carretera Güímar, El Puertito km 1.5** ☎ **922 514530; fax 922 514061**

La Laguna

Nivaria (£)

In a town with few hotels suitable for holidaymakers, the reasonably equipped three-star Aparthotel Nivaria is an acceptable possibility. It has no restaurant but is well placed in the old quarter close to all amenities.

✉ **11 Plaza del Adelantado** ☎ **922 264298**

Santa Cruz de Tenerife

Atlántico (£)

This pleasant, Spanish-oriented hotel is located in the main shopping street at the heart of the city. Defined as a two-star, it is modest and adequately equipped.

✉ **Calle Castillo 12** ☎ **922 246375; fax 922 246378**

Contemporáneo (££)

A modern three-star hotel almost free of English or German voices, located close to the Mencey, the García Sanabria park and the Rambla ring road. There's a restaurant and snack bar.

✉ **Rambla General Franco 116** ☎ **922 271571; fax 922 271223**

Mencey (£££)

Mencey means a Guanche chieftain, and this elegant hotel is the chief among Tenerife's traditional five-star accommodation. In sumptuous colonial style with lavish marble, fine woodwork and artworks on display, the hotel offers every possible amenity. The location is peaceful, away from the city centre on the north side of the Ramblas.

✉ **Avenida Doctor José Naveiras 38** ☎ **922 276700; fax 922 280017**

Pelinor (£)

This is a good example of a smaller, less expensive hotel, located in the heart of the city close to Plaza de España and aimed chiefly at Spanish visitors. Neat, comfortable rooms and there's a bar on the premises.

✉ **Calle Béthencourt Alphonso 8** ☎ **922 246875; fax 922 280520**

Plaza (££)

Located in an agreeable square in the centre of the city, close to shops, restaurants and entertainment, this comfortable, reasonably priced hotel makes a good base in the city.

✉ **Plaza de la Candelaria 10** ☎ **922 272453; fax 922 275160**

Taburiente (££)

An aura of old-world grandeur clings to this long-established, classically furnished hotel. Many of its rooms have attractive views over Parque García Sanabria and the main sights lie within walking distance.

✉ **Avenida Doctor José Naveiras 24A** ☎ **922 276000; fax 922 270562**

The West

Garachico
San Roque (£££)

One of the most unusual and delightful hotels on the island, this historic building stands in the middle of the waterfront. The place has an exquisite low-key elegance. Armchairs and potted plants are dotted about, and there's a lovely arcaded and balconied courtyard within. There are 20 well-equipped rooms.

✉ Calle Esteban de Ponte 32
☎ 922 133435; fax 922 133406

El Tanque
Caserío Los Partidos (£)

This charming little place lies tucked in the hilly terrain of Tenerife's northwest corner, with lovely views towards Pico del Teide. Each bedroom is individually designed with an open fireplace and immaculate bathrooms. Terraces and courtyards bright with flowers and fountains spill around the building. *Tapas* are on the evening menu. This retreat is a long way from the congested coastal resorts and it appeals primarily to walkers and visitors who value peace and quiet. A car is essential if you plan to do any exploring.

✉ El Tanque ☎ 922 693090; fax 922 693138

La Orotava
Victoria (££)

This 17th-century Canarian mansion in the old quarter has been restored in period style. The glass-roofed restaurant is one of its most attractive features, attracting non-residents as well as hotel guests. A roof-top terrace overlooks the valley towards the sea.

✉ Calle Hermano Apolinar 8
☎ 922 331683; fax 922 320519

Los Gigantes
Tamaimo Tropical (££)

This large but secluded complex stands on a quiet site near the Los Gigantes marina and the fine beach of Playa de la Arena. The well-maintained apartment buildings, designed with Canarian-style balconies, shutters and pantiles, are set around two spacious pool terraces with natural shade. Individual units are well-equipped and tastefully decorated with stylish lamps, rugs and tiles. There's a conservatory restaurant, though plenty of eating places lie within walking distance.

✉ Calle Hondura, Puerto de Santiago ☎ 922 860638; fax 922 860761

Parque Nacional del Teide (Teide National Park)
Parador de las Cañadas del Teide (£££)

Tenerife's only *parador* occupies a stunning location near the foot of Pico del Teide and makes an exceptional touring and walking base. Recently refurbished and upgraded, the hotel merges unobtrusively into the surrounding sandy plains and picture windows overlook an array of weirdly eroded rocks. Inside, the hotel is comfortably cheerful, with exposed stonework and open fires to ward off the chill of the altitude. Bedrooms are spacious and well equipped.

✉ Parque Nacional del Teide
☎ 922 386415; fax 922 382352

El Calabazo

Water is scarce on the Canary Islands. To deal with the problem Tenerife farmers used a simple method of scooping water from canals, irrigation ditches or waterways into a tank and taking it to their crops. The men who scooped the water became very skilled, and were called *calabaceros*. The practice died out in the 1970s but *calabazo* contests have become common at fiestas, with contestants seeing how quickly they can transfer water with a scoop. The scoops today are usually metal bowls, but the traditional tool was, of course, a *calabazo* (pumpkin).

Speak the Language?

The official language of the Canary Islands is Castilian Spanish, but the local dialect has many distinguishing features. Most striking is the complete absence of the normal Spanish 'th' sound (as in 'think'), which is usually written as 'ce'. In the Canaries, the letters 'ce' are pronounced as 's'. Another characteristic is the frequent use of Portuguese words, the result of the close relations between the Canaries and Latin America.

Strip off

Topless sunbathing is acceptable at all Tenerife beaches, pools and lidos, especially at the main resorts. Naturism or stripping off completely is never acceptable on resort beaches, but common on any secluded stretch of coast, or beaches outside resorts. Certain hotels at Puerto de la Cruz and Playa de las Américas have secluded separate sunbathing terraces specifically for nude sunbathing

Puerto de la Cruz

Botánico (£££)

An exceptional hotel of relaxed elegance, offering the height of luxury and modern facilities. On the northeast side of town, it's quite a long way from the centre and from the sea. Five stars, and a member of the Leading Hotels of the World group.

✉ **Avenida Richard Yeoward 1, Urbanización Botánico** ☎ 922 381400; fax 922 381504

Marquesa (££)

The waterfront street of the original Puerto saw the creation of this hotel in 1712, long before the advent of tourism. It's been a hotel ever since, still relatively simple, but much modern-ised, with a swimming pool and restaurant. It's thoroughly charming and keeps much of its colonial atmosphere.

✉ **Calle Quintana 11** ☎ 922 383151; fax 922 386950

Monopol (££)

One of the town's earliest hotels, down by the waterfront in the historic quarter. Though much modernised, including the installation of a swimming pool, it retains a pleasing colonial feel, with cane furnishings and greenery in a charming patio.

✉ **Calle Quintana 15** ☎ 922 384611; fax 922 370310

San Felipe (£££)

One of Puerto's best hotels, long established but thoroughly modernised. The high-rise San Felipe is owned by the prestigious Melia group. A huge range of facilities and services is on offer, with children's activities, nightly entertainment and well-equipped rooms. Close to the sea, the hotel is not far from the Playa Martiánez and the promenade, of which it has fine views. The Lago and town centre are only a short stroll away.

✉ **Avenida de Colón 22** ☎ 922 383311; fax 922 373718

San Telmo (£)

Spectacular views of the rocky coast. Though it has nearly a hundred bedrooms, this family-managed hotel still has an intimate, personal feel. The decor combines nautical themes with floral chintz and the restaurant is cosy with wood panelling and fretwork screens. The pool on the rooftop sun terrace is undersized, but it's only a short stroll to the famous Lago. The simple bedrooms are light and spacious with good bathrooms.

✉ **Paseo San Telmo 18** ☎ 922 385853; fax 922 385991

Semiramis (£££)

This ambitious five-star, up the coast from Playa Martiánez, is some distance from the centre of town but has fine sea views from some rooms and offers every modern comfort.

✉ **Leopoldo Cólogan Zulueta 12** ☎ 922 373200; fax 922 373193

Tigaiga (£££)

In the gorgeous garden setting of the Taoro Park area, above the town, this conventional tourist hotel has won awards for its environmental management. One of its claims is that the hotel has more palm trees than beds. Unremarkable but comfortable rooms have partial sea views and face either the Taoro Park or Pico del Teide. The pool area has a view over Puerto and there's a separate terrace for topless sunbathing.

✉ **Parque Taoro 28** ☎ 922 383500; fax 922 384055

The South

Costa Adeje

Colón Guanahani (£££)

An attractive low-rise building in neoclassical style, with marble and columns and arches, this hotel is in the western part of Costa Adeje. Green tile pathways wander among shrubs and palm trees, and the heated seawater pool is pleasant with surrounding trees. There's a good restaurant, plenty of facilities, entertainment and a children's club. Playa de Fañabé is about 150m away.

✉ Calle Bruselas, Playa de Fañabé ☎ 922 712046; fax 922 712121

Gran Hotel Anthelia Park (£££)

This grandiose modern resort complex consists of six small hotel blocks catering to slightly different markets. For example, one is for families, one is quiet, one consists only of luxury suites and so on. All the rooms have a sea view and the whole place is equipped with a wealth of amenities and services. There are five pools, three restaurants, several bars, a kindergarten and a night club, as well as unusual features such as a library. Playa del Duque is a short walk away.

✉ Calle de Londres, Playa del Duque ☎ 922 713335; fax 922 719081

Gran Hotel Bahía del Duque (£££)

One of Tenerife's most extravagant hotels occupies a large secluded plot north of Playa de Fañabe. This elaborate five-star complex consists of some 20 separate, individually designed buildings in Mediterranean and Canarian styles. The reception lobby is an eyecatching space of aviaries, fountains, exotic flowers and murals, and within the beautifully kept grounds the turretted accommodation blocks and multiple restaurants promise a hedonistic stay. Guests enjoy direct access to an immaculate beach boasting an adventurous selection of water sports.

✉ Calle Alcalde Walter Paetzmann s/n ☎ 922 766933; fax 922 746925

Jardín Tropical (£££)

Located at the Puerto Colón end of the Playa de Troya, where Playa de las Américas meets more up-market Costa Adeje, the award-winning Jardín Tropical is a superb resort hotel. Its imaginative white Moorish appearance, beautiful pool area, lush colourful vegetation and seafront location add up to a wonderful, luxurious place to stay on the south coast. There are five restaurants within the hotel.

✉ Calle Gran Bretaña ☎ 922 746000; fax 922 746060

Jardines de Nivaria (£££)

Situated over in the quieter, western end of the resort, near Playa del Duque and Playa de Fañabé, the designers of this hotel have tried to incorporate some local themes into its architecture; tiles and polished wood feature in the rooms. There is an attractive pool area with seawater pools (one heated in winter).

✉ Calle Paris ☎ 922 713333; fax 922 713340

Package Deal

Playa de las Américas, Costa Adeje and Los Cristianos run into each other along the coast, effectively creating a single resort area – often known collectively as Playa de las Américas (► 74). Only Los Cristianos had any existence before the tourism boom took off in the late 1960s. Today the three areas consist almost entirely of scores of hotels, holiday apartments and aparthotels. Almost all visitors arrive on an inclusive package with pre-booked accommodation – and that is the simplest and cheapest way to come to this part of Tenerife. However, the hotels listed here can usually be booked independently, as well as through tour operators.

Class Act

Playa de las Américas has good family accommodation and entertainment but also has its share of bierkellers, lager louts and garish late-night entertainment. Los Cristianos, east of Playa de las Américas, has always been considered a little more select. In contrast to these two, the newer development of Costa Adeje, north of Playa de las Américas, aims to be a little classier, with higher prices, more style, some beautiful landscaping and several modern neoclassical-style hotels.

Golf Coast

Several golf links are located around Playa de las Américas. Just east of the resort the quiet new villa and hotel development of Golf del Sur, though in a rather bleak location close to the former fishing village of Los Abrigos, has the advantage of being only 5km from Reina Sofía Airport and near to high-quality golf links.

Golf del Sur
Las Adelfas (££)

Near Reina Sofía Airport and Los Abrigos village, the aparthotel borders the PGA-approved 27-hole Golf del Sur course. Accommodation is in a cluster of two-storey blocks designed to look like Spanish villas. They have fitted kitchens, simple furnishings and satellite TV, and enclose pools, a restaurant and a bar.

✉ **Urbanización Golf del Sur, San Miguel de Abona exit of Autopista del Sur** ☎ **922 738616; fax 922 738444**

Tenerife Golf (££)

The seafront hotel stands near Reina Sofía Airport, with air-conditioned rooms, all with balcony and cable TV. There's a buffet restaurant, a seawater pool (heated in winter), tennis court and entertainment.

✉ **Urbanización Golf del Sur, San Miguel de Abona exit of Autopista del Sur** ☎ **922 738566; fax 922 738889**

La Escalona
El Nogal (£)

The main attraction of this simple place is its location near Vilaflor, one of the highest and prettiest villages on the island, on the southern approach route to the Teide National Park. Spectacular views over the buckled terrain to Los Cristianos and the Atlantic beyond. A low-key, cream-washed, two-storey building, once part of an 18th-century estate, has been restored to create a small, charming hotel. Neat gardens surround a pool terrace.

✉ **Camino Real** ☎ **922 726050; fax 922 725853**

Los Cristianos
Estefania (£££)

Behind the arid Arona coastline, the road corkscrews steeply upwards into the hills. This elegant retreat rests in a sloping, flower-filled site with extensive views down to the ocean. The shady pool terrace is set with white wicker funiture, and the gardens are landscaped with statuary and fountains. Bedrooms have black Italianate furnishings.

✉ **Urb. Las Aguilas del Teide, Chayofa** ☎ **922 729322; fax 922 751593**

Oasis Moreque (£££)

Inside, this older-style block in the resort centre is rather nicer than its exterior suggests, tastefully decorated in bright, contemporary fabrics and wicker chairs, with a delightful conservatory-style restaurant. Small and friendly, it's popular with families. The rear grounds are pleasing too, with plenty of mature greenery, though not large.

✉ **Avenida Penetración s/n** ☎ **922 790366; fax 922 792260**

Playa de las Américas
Bitácora (££)

One of the big popular holiday hotels, the Bitácora has a spacious pool and lawn, plenty of attractions and facilities for families, and generous buffets.

✉ **Avenida Antonio Domíguez Alfonso 1** ☎ **922 791540; fax 922 796677**

Las Dalias (££)

The huge and popular Las Dalias (800 beds) offers a poolside terrace, paella at the afternoon barbecue and a nightly disco. Nearby Los Hibiscos, Bougainville Playa and Torviscas Playa hotels are similar – all are in the Sungarden group, and all use the same booking numbers.

✉ **Calle Gran Bretaña** ☎ **922 792712; fax 922 797675**

La Gomera

There are only a limited number of hotels and *pensiones* on the island, and most of the accomodation involves staying in homes or private apartments. *Casas rurales* are former farmhouses now converted to rental properties (☎ 922 595019).

Hermigua
Ibo Alfaro (£)
This delightful rural hostelry is on a quiet track above a valley village. The cream-painted 19th-century building has been renovated in traditional Canarian style using natural stone and timber. Breakfast is served on a terrace in fine weather. Bedrooms have tasteful plain walls, wooden shutters and tiled bathrooms.
✉ **Hermigua** ☎ **922 880168; fax 922 881019**

Playa de Santiago
Jardín Tecina (£££)
This top-class hotel in Playa de Santiago clings to a clifftop, with magnificent gardens of native plants (everything is labelled, as in a botanical park). It has a beautiful pool and stirring views over the strait to Tenerife, with Pico del Teide rising in the distance. It's a truly impressive hotel, where the 'rooms' are in delightful cottages in the grounds.
✉ **Lomada de Tecina, Playa de Santiago** ☎ **922 145850; fax 922 145851**

San Sebastián
Parador de San Sebastián de la Gomera (£££)
La Gomera's attractive *parador* stands high above the port up a steeply winding road. The building is a convincing copy of an early colonial mansion. Furnishings are typically Castilian (carved chests and terracotta tiles). Canarian specialities like parrot fish with *mojo* and flambéed bananas feature on the menu. The subtropical clifftop gardens to the rear command views over the town and the local coast, with Pico del Teide visible on neighbouring Tenerife.
✉ **Llano de la Horca 1** ☎ **922 871100; fax 922 871116**

Valle Gran Rey
Jardín del Conde (££)
Low-rise, peach-coloured blocks surround a large pool terrace on the landward side of Valle Gran Rey's promenade. This attractive apartment complex is brightly landscaped with lots of greenery and flowering plants. The one-bedroom apartments all have balconies or terrraces overlooking the pool. A useful mini-market and bar is located near the entrance and there are plenty of eating places nearby.
✉ **Avenida Maritima** ☎ **922 806008; fax 922 805385**

Vallehermoso
Hotel de Triana (£)
A picturesque village. The plain exterior of this modest house in a residential street belies its contemporary decor of cool, soothing colours, plain walls and exposed stonework. Bedrooms feature mosaic-tiled bathrooms, and some have kitchenettes. A small restaurant provides simple, home-cooked cuisine.
✉ **Calle Triana** ☎ **922 800528; fax 922 800128**

On the Cards
Credit cards are widely accepted in both large and small shops in Santa Cruz, Puerto de la Cruz and the Playa de las Américas area. In other towns, and all over La Gomera, expect to be told only cash is acceptable.

Children's Attractions

Home from Home
Families with young children should consider self-catering in preference to hotel accommodation. Tenerife has plenty of holiday apartments and aparthotels, combining small self-catering suites with some hotel facilities. London-based Casas Canarias specialises in self-catering accommodation (☎ 020 74854387).

The island provides little that is especially for children, but it doesn't need to – most of Tenerife's attractions are a are a big hit with people of all ages.

Amazing Plants
Plant life in Tenerife is not just of interest to gardeners – some of it is weird enough even to grab the attention of children.

Bananera El Guanche
All about bananas – and other plants (► 55).
✉ 2km from Puerto de la Cruz, on road to La Orotava ☎ 922 331853 ⏰ Daily 9–6

Drago Milenario
One of the largest and oldest specimens of this curious tree (► 17).
✉ Icod de los Vinos 🚌 354, 363 from Puerto de la Cruz

Jardín Botánico
Spot the giant South American fig tree in this exotic garden (► 58).
✉ Calle Retama 2, off Carretara del Botánico, Puerto de la Cruz ☎ 922 383572 ⏰ Summer, daily 9–7; winter, 9–6

Jardines del Atlántico Bananera
Another chance to go bananas at these lush gardens on Tenerife's south coast.
✉ Exit 26 of Autopista del Sur ☎ 922 720403 ⏰ Tours at 10, 11:30, 1, 2:15 and 3:30

Parque Nacional de Garajonay
The twisting branches of the forest are like scenes from a movie (► 26).
✉ La Gomera

Animal Parks
Loro Parque
A tropical wonderland of animals and birds, including parrots, gorillas, tigers, monkeys, penguins, flamingos and performing dolphins (► 21).
✉ 1.5km west of Puerto de la Cruz, near Punta Brava ☎ 922 373841 ⏰ Daily 8:30–5 🚌 Free shuttle from Avenida de Colón (near Lago) and Plaza del Charco, Puerto de la Cruz

Oasis del Valle
Canarian flora and fauna and other friendly creatures set in lush subtropical gardens in the Orotava Valley
✉ El Ramal 35, La Orotava (Exit 33 from Autopista del Norte) ☎ 922 333509 ⏰ Daily 10–5 🚌 Free bus from Playa de Martiánez (near Lago), Puerto de la Cruz

Parque Ecológico Aguilas del Teide
See condors and crocodiles, tigers, eagles and penguins in this dramatic tropical park, where in five display areas creatures put on regular performances. Feeding times are particularly worth seeing. Also on the site dodgem boats and other amusements (► 75).
✉ On Arona road 3km from Los Cristianos ☎ 922 753001 ⏰ Summer, daily 9–6; winter, 10–6 🚌 Free shuttle bus from Playa de las Américas and Los Cristianos

Parques Exóticos
Cactus and animal park, and also a reptilarium (► 78).
✉ Near Exit 26 of Autopista del Sur ☎ 922 795424 ⏰ Daily 10–6 🚌 Free shuttle bus from Playa de las Américas and Los Cristianos

Tenerife Zoo

Apes, lions, crocodiles and many other creatures.

✉ Llano Azul, Arona (Exit 26 of Autopista del Sur) ☎ 922 790720 🕐 Daily 9:30–6 🚌 Free shuttle bus from southern resorts

Camel Rides
Camel Park

A farm in the sun, breeding camels, making wine, growing local crops and selling island crafts. One of their principal activities is mini-excursions by camel.

✉ Exit 27 of Autopista del Sur ☎ 922 721080 🕐 Daily 10–5 🚌 Free shuttle bus from Los Cristianos and Playa de las Américas

Camello Center

Hold on tight for camel rides and donkey safaris at El Tanque, near Garachico. Afterwards have tea in an Arab tent.

✉ El Tanque (east of Garachico) ☎ 922 136399 🕐 Daily 10–6

Eating Out

Children are welcome in bars and restaurants. However, restaurants, bars and cafés don't generally list children's menus or provide dishes specially for children – instead, they are given small portions of whatever they fancy.

Fiesta Magic

Come to Tenerife during the Santa Cruz carnival (early to mid-Feb) for a wild week of mayhem and all-night revelry that will thrill older children (though might not appeal to younger ones). Failing that, find a fiesta during your visit – the noise, amusements, music and crowds provide unforgettable memories.

Meeting Whales and Dolphins

Whale- and dolphin-watching is one of the most popular activities on Tenerife. About 20 different species of sea mammals live in Canary Island waters, mostly off the west coast of Tenerife between Los Cristianos and Los Gigantes. Glass-bottomed boats offer a chance to spot other marine life too.

Under the Sea
Yellow Submarine

A submarine adventure takes you exploring among the depths of the sea.

✉ South Pier, Puerto Colón, Playa de las Américas ☎ 922 715080 🕐 Hourly trips 10–4 🚌 Free shuttle bus from southern resorts and Aquapark

Water Fun
Aquapark

This water amusement park offers slides, pools, dolphin shows and water features. Plan to spend at least half a day; you can have a meal here too (▶ 74).

✉ San Eugenio Alto, Costa Adeje/Playa de las Américas (Exit 29 of Autopista del Sur) ☎ 922 715266 🕐 Daily 10–6 🚌 Free shuttle bus from southern resorts

Small World
Pueblo Chico

Models of Canarian landscapes and buildings are carefully reproduced to a scale of 1:25 in this large open-air attraction in the hills behind Puerto de la Cruz.

✉ Valle de la Orotava ☎ 922 334060

On Film

Teide National Park (▶ 66) is a good choice for a day out with young movie buffs. Intended to convey a primeval wilderness, it has featured as a background in *The Ten Commandments* and *Planet of the Apes*. In the film *One Million Years BC*, Raquel Welch appeared here wearing only a fur bikini.

Handicrafts & Souvenirs

A Taste of Honey
One of the strangest specialities of the Canary Islands is the palm-tree 'honey' of La Gomera. Not real honey, *miel de palma* is made like maple syrup. The *guarapo*, or sap, of the date palm is tapped, then boiled. The result is a dark syrup, rich, tasty and sweet. Buy it where you see signs at smallholdings around the island, or in the market at San Sebastián.

Duty and Tax
Although the Canary Islands are a duty-free area, it doesn't follow that all goods are free of tax. Prices are bumped up by the local IGIC tax, which puts 5 per cent on the value of goods and is sometimes not included in window-display prices.

Embroidery, Lace and Threadwork
The Canaries are known for exquisite embroidery (*bordados*) and fine threadwork (*calados*), and decorative lacework, especially doilies (*rosetas*). Exceptional patience, skill, delicacy and care are required of the local women who do the work. However, you should beware of street sellers and market traders offering very inferior low-priced imported factory-made embroidery and claiming that it is genuine local craftwork.

Pottery
Canarian potters traditionally didn't use the potter's wheel, and on Tenerife and La Gomera highly skilled local potters still work by hand to produce distinctive household objects and decorative items (▶ 84). Look out in the craft shops for their *gánigos* – household pots made without a potter's wheel – and necklaces and other jewellery decorated with Guanche symbols.

Wickerwork
Local handmade Tenerife basketwork is distinctive and pretty, and makes a good choice for souvenirs. Skilled wickerwork craftsmen and women can be seen working in the many craft fairs.

Shops
A range of all these locally made items can be found at the following craft stores. It may be worth shopping around, as the stock varies from place to place. Shop hours are generally Mon–Sat 9–1, 4–8.

The North
Arte Tenerife
✉ Plaza de España, Santa Cruz

Artesanía Celsa
✉ Calle Castillo 8, Santa Cruz

Casa de los Balcones
✉ Edificio Olympo, Plaza de la Candelaria, Santa Cruz

Casa de los Calados
✉ Calle Núñez de la Peña 9, La Laguna

Mercado de Artesanía Española
✉ Plaza de la Candelaria 8, Santa Cruz

The West
Artesanía del Lino
✉ Calle Santo Domingo, Puerto de la Cruz

Casa de los Balcones
This beautifully restored 17th-century mansion (▶ 16) contains a craft shop where local people can often be seen at work. As well as inexpensive souvenirs, a wide range of high-quality items, such as Spanish and Canarian lace and linen and traditional Canarian embroideries, are on sale. Some are made on the premises, as the Casa de los Balcones also serves as a highly regarded school of embroidery.
✉ Calle San Francisco 3, La Orotava

Casa de los Balcones
✉ Paseo de San Telmo 22, Puerto de la Cruz

Casa del Turista
Located opposite La Orotava's famous Casa de los Balcones (► 108), this craft and souvenir shop has the same owners and stocks similar products.
✉ Calle San Francisco 4, La Orotava

Casa Iriarte
The disorganised store in this historic building has a fine selection of hand-worked table linen.
✉ Calle San Juan 17, Puerto de la Cruz

Casa Torrehermosa
This is run by the state-run crafts organisation, Empresa Insular de Artesanía del Cabildo de Tenerife, and specialises in genuine local work. There is a craft museum attached.
✉ Calle Tomás Zerolo 27, La Orotava ☎ 922 334013

Centro Artesanal El Limonero
✉ Avenida Tome Cano, Garachico

The South
Canaria Océano
✉ Carretera General de Chío, Guía de Isora

Casa de los Balcones
A wide range of inexpensive crafts.
✉ Gran Hotel Bahía del Duque Fañabe, Costa Adeje

Mercado de Artesanía Española
An interesting stop on the way into the Teide National Park.
✉ Carretera General, Vilaflor

La Gomera
Artesanía Los Telares
See weaving and other local crafts in production before you buy. There is a similar *artesanía* at Agulo, the next village about 3km away.
✉ Hermigua ⏰ Mon–Sat

Market
Gomeran craftwork and local products at the morning market.
✉ Avenida de Colón, San Sebastián

Summer Fairs
Have fun while looking for souvenirs at these summer fairs, or *ferias artesanía*.

Los Realejos	May, Jun
Güimar	Jun
La Orotava	Jun
El Sauzal	Jun/Jul
La Laguna	Jul
Santiago del Teide	Jul
Arona/Los Cristianos	Jul/Aug
Fasnia	Aug
El Rosario	Aug
Garachico	Aug
La Victoria de Acentejo	Aug
Buenavista del Norte	Aug
La Matanza	Aug
Vilaflor	Aug/Sep
San Juan de la Rambla	Sep
San Miguel de Abona	Sep
Guía de Isora	Sep
Tacoronte	Sep
El Tanque	Oct

Unusual Souvenirs
Choose from banana-shaped bottles of sugary *cobana* (banana liqueur), dolls in national costume, items made from palm leaves, or banana-leaf baskets. Also woodcarving, leatherware, prettily packaged sweets and biscuits or bottles of spicy *mojo* sauce, local wines, cigars or plant souvenirs like baby dragon trees, and bird-of-paradise flowers are all worth looking out for.

Gomeran Pots
La Gomera continues traditional methods of making handmade pots without a potter's wheel. One of the villages best known for this is tiny El Cercado, high on a narrow, winding road in the west of the island (► 84). Many of its simple cottages are pottery workshops, where the pots are made from the island's striking dark red clay.

Bargains and Markets

Out of Africa

Colourfully dressed West Africans hawking on the beaches, in the streets and selling in the markets and fairs of Tenerife add an exotic note. These traders are often Senegalese, make the boat trip specifically to sell in European markets and stay for several months. Usually they all sell very similar goods: leatherwork, carved toys, African drums, beads and, at higher prices, often illegally exported tribal artefacts, including ceremonial masks. Do not to buy ivory – many African traders offer ivory items, but these are illegal throughout the EU, with heavy fines and confiscation of the goods if found by customs officers.

Hypermarket Shopping

Self-caterers and others will sometimes prefer to go to a supermarket to make shopping easy. The Continente *centro comercial* not only has a huge hypermarket with a vast range of goods at reasonable prices, but there are over 100 other shops on the site. The Continente is 5km south of Santa Cruz by the Santa Maria del Mar exit of the Autopista del Sur (Mon–Sat 10–10).

Bargains

As a duty-free region, the Canary Islands are like a big duty-free shop, selling perfumes, cameras, binoculars and other optical goods, CD players and electronic goods, at lower prices than at home (▶ 108).

In the big towns and main resorts, several Asian–run 'Bazaars' are the usual outlet for these goods. Marked prices are generally open to a bit of haggling, though some stores make a point of not negotiating – a selling point with Europeans who dread haggling! Prices are similar to those in airport shops and other duty-free outlets. Before buying, it helps to know what the price is back home and whether the guarantee will be valid. The main outlets are Calle de Castillo, Santa Cruz; Playa de las Américas; and Puerto de la Cruz.

Markets and Hawkers

Genuine markets like Mercado Nuestra Señora de África in Santa Cruz (▶ 23) are the place to find fresh fruit and vegetables, kitchenware, fabrics and household items.

Most other Tenerife markets attract European hippy 'artists' and African traders, selling a repetitive range of kitsch, beads and home-made jewellery, and leather goods. Some of them occasionally offer original or interesting items. They are often joined by Spanish stallholders offering either bargain clothes and beachwear, or lace, crochet and embroidery, especially tablecloths, placemats, napkins, bedlinen and handkerchiefs. These are not always offered at low prices, but they represent good value for such high-quality handmade work. You may also find glazed pottery and crockery, attractively hand-painted. When not at the markets, the hippies and African traders often hawk their goods in streets and on the beaches.

Main Markets

Los Abrigos
Night market
 Tue 6–10

Los Cristianos
 Next to Hotel Arona Gran
 Sun 9–2

Playa de las Américas
 Torviscas
 Thu, Sat 9–2

Puerto de la Cruz
Mercado Municipal San Felipe
 Avenida de Blas Pérez Gonzáles   Mon–Sat AM

Santa Cruz
Mercado Nuestra Señora de África
 Just off Calle de San Sebastián   Mon–Sat 8–1

Rastro **(flea market)**
 Near the *mercado*, Calle José Manuel Guimerá
 Sun 10–2

San Sebastián, La Gomera
 Avenida de Colón
 Mon–Sat AM

Tacoronte
Farmers' market
 Sat PM, Sun AM

Excursions

Arts and Drama

Tenerife has several art galleries, museums, concert halls and theatres. Most of the island's culture is firmly located in the north, well away from the tourist sites.

La Laguna

The town of La Laguna, little frequented by tourists, is Tenerife's centre of contemporary culture.

Teatro Leal

Hosts annual festivals of jazz, folk music and international theatre.
✉ **Calle Obispo Rey Redondo**

Santa Cruz
Auditorio

A state-of-the-art concert hall opened in 2002.
✉ **Near the Parque Marítimo César Manrique**

Teatro Guimerá

Plays (Spanish-language only), opera and concerts – and home of the first-class Symphony Orchestra of Tenerife, which gives performances all year.
✉ **Plaza Isla de la Madera**
☎ **922 606265**

Boat Excursions

Many tour operators and local travel firms organise boat excursions from Los Cristianos, Playa de las Américas, Costa Adeje and Costa del Silencio. Day trips to La Gomera are especially popular and enjoyable. Other boat trips have no goal except fun, such as the many *sangréa* excursions and pirate adventures, which include lunch and usually a swimming stop.

Yellow Submarine

A trip in a semi-submersible to explore the seas around southern Tenerife (► 107).
✉ **South Pier, Puerto Colón, Playa de las Américas** ☎ **922 715080** 🕐 **Hourly trips 10–4**

Tours

Organised bus or coach tours are a popular way of exploring the landscapes of Tenerife. See panel, Coach Tours, for suggestions.

Whalewatching

About 200 pilot whales live in the Canary Island waters, usually on the south side of the archipelago. An easy place to spot whales is between Los Cristianos and Los Gigantes; dolphins can also be found. Boat trips to see them are among the highlights for visitors.

Nostramo

Successful and popular boat excursions in a beautiful Spanish schooner built in 1918. As well as seeing dolphins and whales, the leisurely outing is unforgettable for the lunch below the Los Gigantes cliffs and a pause in Masca Bay for a chance to swim.
✉ **Playa San Juan, Playa de las Américas** ☎ **922 750085 (Playa de las Américas), 922 385116 (Puerto de la Cruz)** 🕐 **Departs daily 10AM** 🚌 **Free bus from southern resorts**

Tropical Delfin

Modern excursion boat with underwater windows to view the sea life.
✉ **South Pier, Puerto Colón, Playa de las Américas** ☎ **922 750149** 🕐 **Daily trips 10:30, 1:30**

Coach Tours

The most rewarding tours include a trip to Pico del Teide; across the Macizo de Teno to Masca; and a day out in Santa Cruz. If you are staying in Playa de las Américas a day trip to Puerto de la Cruz, including Loro Parque and Bananera El Guanche, is highly enjoyable. Another worthwhile tour is the day out on La Gomera. These tours are available from hotel reception desks and through tour operators' reps at the resorts.

Whalewatching Tips

• Only travel with boat firms licensed to run excursions (like the two included on this page).
• Boats should not get too close to whales.
• Engines should be turned off when near whales.
• Don't change direction frequently – this irritates the whales.
• Don't throw anything at whales (and do not throw litter into the sea).
• Don't swim with whales – remember, they are wild animals.

Sport

Peaceful Island
In contrast to the lively scene on its larger neighbour, little La Gomera has almost no organised sport, entertainment or nightlife. Some of the hotels do put on low-key shows, and there are small discos. Tourists, like locals, must rely on fiestas for music, folklore and fun.

Golf
Many visitors come to Tenerife just to play on the excellent golf courses, four of which are in the area between Playa de las Américas and Reina Sofía Airport. If you are playing and staying in the south, visit the northern golf course at least once – for the amazing contrast of lush greenery. Each of the golf courses has formed partnerships with nearby hotels, whose resident guests enjoy reduced green fees (enquire at the clubs for details).

North
Real Club de Golf Tenerife
An 18-hole course founded in 1932 by British expatriates.
✉ **El Peñon, Tacoronte, 2km from Los Rodeos Airport, 14km from Santa Cruz**
☎ **922 636607,**
www.realgolfdetenerife.com

South
Amarilla Golf
An 18-hole course beside coastal cliffs.
✉ **Urbanización Amarilla Golf, San Miguel de Abona** ☎ **922 730319**

Golf del Sur
This 27-hole course has hosted several international events.
✉ **Urbanización Golf del Sur, San Miguel de Abona** ☎ **922 738170**

Costa Adeje Golf
This fine 27-hole course has greens with several doglegs. Located 5km from Playa de las Américas, with views of La Gomera.
✉ **Finca de los Olivos, Adeje** ☎ **922 710000**

Golf Las Américas
A 72-par course just outside Playa de las Américas and Los Cristianos; 18 holes.
✉ **Exit 28 of Autopista del Sur**
☎ **922 752005**

Centro de Golf Los Palos
A par-27 nine-hole course, just 6km east of Playa de las Américas. Small but plenty of challenges.
✉ **Carretera Guaza–Las Galletas km 7, Arona** ☎ **922 169080**

Water Sports
Scuba and offshore diving is popular all around the islands. Several centres offer a good standard and are staffed by qualified instructors. Diving courses should meet PADI standards and also check insurance cover.

Barlovento
Canoeing, sailing, water-skiing, windsurfing and boat hire.
✉ **Parque Marítino César Manrique, Santa Cruz** ☎ **922 223840**

Centro de Buceo Atlantik
✉ **Hotel Maritim, Calle El Burgado 1, Puerto de la Cruz**
☎ **922 362801**

Centro Insular de Deportes Marinos (CIDEMAT)
Canoeing, diving, sailing, water-skiing and windsurfing.
✉ **Carretera Santa Cruz–San Andrés** ☎ **922 240945**

Club Nautico
✉ **Avenida de Anaga, Santa Cruz** ☎ **922 240945**

Nautiocio
Jet skiing, parascending,

sailing, water-skiing and banana boats.

✉ **Puerto Colón, Costa Adeje**
☎ 922 714034

Sunwind

Near-constant trade winds and warm unpolluted waters ensure ideal conditions for windsurfing and surfing around the island's south coast. One of the best locations is El Médano beach, close to Reina Sofía Airport. Waters on the north coast are too rough for safe surfing.

✉ **Avenida Islas Canarias, El Médano** ☎ 922 176174

Go-Karting
Karting Club Tenerife

This club has one of the best kart circuits in Europe.

✉ **Carretera de Cho, at km 66, off the southern Autopista at Guaza** ☎ 922 786620

Walking, Climbing, Cycling

Graded footpaths marked and maintained by ICONA, the Spanish conservation agency, criss-cross the island. The agency issues a number of maps (available in tourist offices and park visitor centres on the island) showing marked walks. These include a pocket-size pack of 22 different footpath maps, with descriptions in English and some history about each area and the landmarks, flora and fauna. Discovery Walking Guides and Sunflower Guides (available in the UK) are useful additions aimed at the walker. See panel, right.

Aden Tenerife MultiAventura

This highly proficient multi-adventure sports centre organises cycling tours, mountain cycling, horse riding, walking excursions and climbing.

✉ **Calle Castillo (Oficina 307) 41, Santa Cruz** ☎ 922 246261

Gaiatours

A well-know trekking operator offering a regular weekly programme of guided walks in interesting parts of Tenerife.

☎ 922 355272

Gregorio

An established escort walks specialist, offering over 50 routes for all ages and fitness levels.

✉ **Hotel Tigaiga, Parque Taoro 28, Puerto de la Cruz** ☎ 922 383500

Wrestling

One of the traditional island sports, called *la lucha* or *lucha canaria*, is a curious form of wrestling. With its own weekly TV show and frequent matches, Canarian wrestling has become very popular in recent years. Two teams compete by pitting one man against another, in turns, until there is a clear victory. The men, wearing a particular style of shorts and shirt, try to throw each other to the ground by gripping the side of each other's clothing. It is slow and careful, with sudden moves as the men try to catch each other off guard. Tourists are welcome to watch matches; ask at hotels or tourist office for match details and venues. Demonstrations are given at the Hotel Tigaiga:

✉ **Parque Taoro 28, Puerto de la Cruz** ☎ 922 383500
🕐 **Sun 11AM**

Walking Advice

ICONA, the Spanish conservation agency, gives the following advice to walkers in Tenerife:
• Take a hat and sunglasses
• Take water to drink
• Don't pick any plants
• Let someone know about your walk
• Never walk without a map (available from Puerto de la Cruz and Santa Cruz tourist offices, and Teide National Park Visitor Centre (☎ 922 290129)

Nightlife

A Night In
Most tourist hotels, especially the larger places, offer music, shows and entertainment on the premises every evening. Some can be quite spectacular, with a cabaret-style floorshow and dancers. Flamenco and colourful folk shows are common. Several hotels also host loud, atmospheric discos for the younger crowd.

Champion Cocktail
Puerto de la Cruz's Casino Taoro won the 1988 Spanish National Cocktail Contest for its house drink, called Cocktail Taoro. It's a sizzling, hilarious, extravagant and drinkable mix of champagne, calvados and banana liqueur with lemon and caviar.

Casinos

Casino Playa de las Américas
Place your bets at the Hotel Gran Tinerfe.
✉ **Avenida Rafael Puig Llurina, Playa de las Américas** ☎ **922 793758** 🕐 From 7PM

Casino Santa Cruz
Dress up for an evening of roulette, blackjack and poker at Tenerife's poshest hotel.
✉ **Hotel Mencey, Avenida Doctor José Naveiras 38, Santa Cruz** ☎ **922 276700** 🕐 From 8PM

Casino Taoro
Tenerife's grandest casino, in Puerto de la Cruz, is housed in a former hotel that played host to Europe's nobility over a century ago. Although badly damaged by fire in 1929, the hotel's lavish architecture and wonderful location high in the Parque Taoro guaranteed its survival, and it reopened as a casino. Cocktails are served, there is a restaurant, and slot machines as well as roulette and gambling tables. Casual dressers are not admitted, there's a modest entrance charge, and you must take your passport.
✉ **Parque Taoro, Puerto de la Cruz** ☎ **922 380550** 🕐 From 8PM

Pubs, Clubs and Discos

Los Cristianos/Playa de las Américas

Las Veronicas, on the seafront road in Playa de las Américas is the focal point for entertainment. Things liven up around 11PM, bars close 3AM–6AM.

Aquarium
✉ **Avenida de Suecia, Los Christianos**

Banana Garden
A (slightly) older group prefers this show, restaurant and music venue.
✉ **Veronicas, Playa de las Américas** ☎ **922 790365**

Byblos
✉ **Hotel Columbus, Playa de las Américas**

Linekers Bar
Booze, telly, bar food and good cheer at this noisily popular laddish football pub opposite Las Veronicas.
✉ **Centro Comercial Starco, Playa de las Américas**

Metropolis
There's a young party atmosphere at this popular pub-disco. Two rooms – one for house, and the other for live music and disco.
✉ **Hotel Conquistador, Paseo Maritimo, Playa de las Américas** ☎ **922 797359**

Prismas
✉ **Hotel Tenerife Sol, Playa de las Américas** ☎ **922 790371**

Trauma
✉ **Centro Comercial Palm Beach, Avenida Litoral, Playa de las Américas** ☎ **922 790001**

Puerto de la Cruz

A quieter, slightly older holiday crowd frequents Puerto's late night venues.

Blue Note
A well-known jazz spot.
✉ **Calle Zamora 15**

Qatar
✉ **Calle Aceviño, Urbanización La Paz**

Concordia Club
✉ Avenida de Venezuela 3

Joy
✉ Obispo Pérez Cáceres

Victoria
✉ Hotel Tenerife Playa,
Avenida de Colón

Santa Cruz

The clientele who jam into Santa Cruz's nightspots are mainly young Spanish visitors, and the more adventurous among the foreign tourists.

Daida
✉ Calle Carlos Hamilton, Residencial Anaga

Ku
✉ Parque la Granja

Nooctua
✉ Avenida Anaga 37

Dinner Dance, Nightclubs and Cabaret

Known here as 'show restaurants', many places offer different styles of floorshows and entertainment while the audience is dining or drinking. Some are very slick, featuring international comedians, jugglers and other entertainers. Others offer a more risqué type of performance, with the prettiest of showgirls dressed in feathers and not much else.

Barbacoa Tacorante
Folklore show based on Tenerife's carnival. Colourful costumes and a barbecue style dinner.
✉ Calle Garoé, Urbanización La Paz, Peurto de la Cruz
☎ 922 382910

Puerto de la Cruz and the West

Andromeda
This popular, stylish cabaret and show restaurant was created by artist César Manrique and is located at the Lago Martiánez on the seafront. It attracts world-class artistes and highly professional dancers and showgirls.
✉ Isla del Lago, Lago Martiánez, Puerto de la Cruz
☎ 922 383852 🕐 Dinner 8PM, floor show 10PM

Barbacoa Tacorante
Folklore show based on Tenerife's carnival. Colourful costumes and a barbecue-style dinner.
✉ Calle Garoé, Urbanización La Paz, Peurto de la Cruz
☎ 922 382910

Tenerife Palace
✉ Camino del Coche, Puerto de la Cruz ☎ 922 382960

Playa de las Américas and the South

La Ballena
A show-restaurant in Ten-Bel, on the Costa del Silencio.
✉ Ten-Bel ☎ 922 730060

Pirámides de Arona
Ambitious gala performances featuring cabaret, opera, ballet and flamenco.
✉ Mare Nostrum Resort, Avenida de las Américas, Playa de las Américas ☎ 922 757549

Tablao Flamenco
See flamenco shows while you dine.
✉ Avenida Rafael Puig Lluvina, Playa de las Américas
☎ 922 797611

Theme Dinners

Castillo San Miguel
You can pretend it's the Middle Ages in this mock-medieval castle. Dine in jolly mood to the accompaniment of tournaments and boisterous family fun with music, singing and dancing.
✉ Aldea Blanca, San Miguel
☎ 922 700276

A Night on the Town

In Puerto de la Cruz, nightlife is mainly focused on Avenida de Colón and its side turnings. It's relaxed, good-humoured and civilised, with live music bars and discos. In Playa de las Américas, things are livelier, more raucous and harder-edged, with the centre of action being around the Veronicas complex. Here you'll find discos for all tastes, and fun pubs and bars where things get going after 11PM. To get away from tourists, visit Santa Cruz for cheaper discos and late-night bars – look along Avenida Anaga and Rambla del General Franco. Don't miss the city's open-air discos during high summer. However, Santa Cruz tends to be quiet at night during the week, livelier at weekends.

What's On When

Spit out the Old Year, Swallow the New

Locals have their own tradition, which is fun to share if you are here on New Year's Eve. As the clock strikes midnight and the new year begins, at every chime you should eat a grape and spit the seeds out. If you can do that without difficulty, you should also take a sip of *cava* at every one of the 12 chimes.

Carnival Month

The high point of the year for most Tenerife residents is the wild, colourful and sometimes frenzied week-long carnival in February. It's the second biggest carnival in the world after Rio and draws immense crowds from all Spanish-speaking countries. The high point is Shrove Tuesday. Huge processions and parades, with participants dressed in fantastic costumes that have often taken the whole year to prepare, take over the capital city and to a lesser extent Tenerife's other big towns. The whole month is affected, as people take time off work to prepare, to celebrate – or to recover from staying up all night and enjoying drinks like the carnival favourite, Cubata – rum and Coke.

January
Cabalgata de los Reyes Magos (The Three Kings Cavalcade, 5–6 Jan): many places, especially Santa Cruz and Valle Gran Rey (La Gomera)
Fiestas (17–22 Jan): Garachico, Icod de los Vinos, Los Realejos and San Sebastián (La Gomera)

February
The whole month is called Carnival Month, with a festive mood everywhere.
Candelaria (Candlemas, 2 Feb): big festival and pilgrimage in certain towns and villages, especially Candelaria
Carnaval (one week around 8–15 Feb): Santa Cruz and Puerto de la Cruz – huge events, parades, festivities. The climax is Shrove Tuesday, the biggest event of the year.
Carnaval (end Feb): Los Cristianos – marks the end of Tenerife's Carnival Month
Carnaval (end Feb/early Mar): San Sebastián (La Gomera)

March/April
San José holiday (19 Mar)
Semana Santa (Holy Week): big events, often sober in character, all over the islands during Easter Week
Fiestas (25 Apr): especially at Icod de los Vinos, Teguesta and Agulo (La Gomera)

May/June
Día de las Islas Canarias (Canary Islands Day, 30 May): throughout the archipelago
Corpus Christi (late May/early Jun, c2 Jun): Octavo (8 days) of huge celebrations throughout the island, especially La Orotava, La Laguna and Vilaflor. Streets are decorated with sand-and-flower designs.
Romería (after Corpus Christi): the season of local pilgrimages
Fiesta de San Juan (24 Jun): midsummer celebrated at Vallehermoso (La Gomera) and other villages

July
Fiestas del Gran Poder (15 Jul): Puerto de la Cruz – processions, parades, fireworks and fun
Santiago (25 Jul): festive public holiday; Santa Cruz, celebration of the defeat of Rear Admiral Nelson (1797)

August
Asunción and Nuestra Señora de la Candelaria (15 Aug): Candelaria – important pilgrimage festival involving the whole of Tenerife
Romería de San Roque (16 Aug): Garachico – popular, colourful local event
Nuestra Señora del Carmen (30 Aug): Los Cristianos – lively fiesta

September
Semana Colombina (Columbus Week, 1–6 Sep): San Sebastián (La Gomera)
Virgen de Buen Paso (15 Sep): Alajeró (La Gomera)
Fiestas (mid-Sep): La Laguna and Tacoronte

October
Día de la Hispanidad (12 Oct): celebrating Columbus
Fiesta de los Cacharros (Pots and Pans, 29 Oct): noisy fiesta to celebrate the arrival of the new wine

November/December
Holidays (1 Nov, 6 Dec, 8 Dec, 25 Dec)

Practical Matters

Above: *windsurfing at El Médano*
Right: *a timeshare salesperson on the move*

117

TIME DIFFERENCES

GMT	Tenerife	California	USA (NY)	New Zealand	Spain
Noon	Noon	← 4 AM	← 7 AM	→ Midnight	→ 1 PM

BEFORE YOU GO

WHAT YOU NEED

● Required ○ Suggested ▲ Not required	Some countries require a passport to remain valid for a minimum period (usually at least six months) beyond the date of entry – contact their consulate or embassy or your travel agent for details.	UK	Germany	USA	Netherlands	Spain
Passport		●	●	●	●	●
Visa (regulations can change – check before booking your trip)		▲	▲	▲	▲	▲
Onward or Return Ticket		●	●	○	●	●
Health Inoculations		▲	▲	▲	▲	▲
Health Documentation (► 123, Health)		▲	▲	▲	▲	▲
Travel Insurance		○	○	○	○	○
Driving Licence (national)		●	●	●	●	●
Car Insurance Certificate (if own car)		●	●	●	●	●
Car Registration Document (if own car)		●	●	●	●	●

WHEN TO GO

Tenerife

▮▮▮▮▮ High season

▭▭▭▭▭ Low season

20°C	21°C	23°C	24°C	25°C	27°C	28°C	29°C	28°C	26°C	23°C	20°C
JAN	FEB	MAR	APR	MAY	JUN	JUL	AUG	SEP	OCT	NOV	DEC

 Very wet   Wet   Cloud   Sun   Coud/Sun

TOURIST OFFICES

In the UK
Spanish National Tourist Office
22–23 Manchester Square
London W1M 5AP
☎ 020 74868077

In the USA
Tourist Office of Spain
666 Fifth Avenue, 35th floor
New York, NY 10103
☎ 212 265-8822

Other TOs in Chicago,
Los Angeles, Miami.

WHEN YOU ARE THERE

ARRIVING

By Air Almost all flights to Tenerife arrive at Reina Sofía (or Tenerife Sur) Airport (☎ 922 759200), on the Costa del Silencio near Playa de las Américas in the south of the island. A second airport, Los Rodeos or Tenerife Norte (☎ 922 6359880), at La Laguna in the north of the island, is used for domestic inter-island flights. Flights to La Gomera will eventually use a new airport at Playa de Santiago in the south of the island, but at present services are restricted.

By Sea It is possible for independent travellers to reach the islands on a slow boat from Cadiz, on the Spanish mainland. The journey takes around two days. Inter-island ferries and hydrofoils connect Tenerife and La Gomera to the other islands.

Reina Sofía Airport to:	Journey times
Puerto de la Cruz: 100km 	2 hours
Playa de las Américas: 15km	25 minutes

MONEY

The euro is the single currency of the European Monetary Union, which has been adopted by 12 member states including Spain. Euro banknotes and coins were introduced in January 2002. There are banknotes for 5, 10, 20, 50, 100, 200 and 500 euros, and coins for 1, 2, 5, 10, 20 and 50 cents, and 1 and 2 euros. Euro traveller's cheques are widely accepted.

TIME

 The time in Tenerife (and all the Canary Islands) is the same as in the UK. Sometimes a temporary 1-hour time difference occurs when clocks go forward or back in March and September. The Canary Islands are 5 hours ahead of the eastern US.

CUSTOMS

YES

There are no restrictions at all on goods taken into Tenerife or other Canary Islands.
It would be pointless to take most goods into these islands in the expectation of saving money, however, as almost everything is cheaper in the Canaries than it is at home. If you are carrying a large amount of money, you should declare it on arrival to avoid explanations on departure.

NO
There are a few obvious exceptions to the information above, notably illegal drugs, firearms, obscene material and unlicensed animals.

EMBASSIES AND CONSULATES

UK
Santa Cruz
☎ 922 286863

USA
Santa Cruz
☎ 922 286950

Germany
Santa Cruz
☎ 922 284812

Canada
Madrid
☎ 91 4314556

WHEN YOU ARE THERE

TOURIST OFFICES

● **Tenerife**
Garachico
Calle Estéban de Ponte 5
☎ 922 133461

Los Cristianos
Centro Cultural, Plaza del
Carmen
☎ 922 757137

Los Gigantes
Edificio Seguro del Sol
36–37, Playa de la Arena
☎ 922 860348

Playa de las Américas
Centro Comercial City
Centre
☎ 922 797668

Puerto de la Cruz
Plaza de Europa 5
☎ 922 386000

Santa Cruz
Palacio Insular (ground
floor), Plaza de España
☎ 922 239592

● **La Gomera**
Playa de Santiago
Edificio Las Vistas, Local 8,
Avenida Marítima
☎ 922 895650

San Sebastián
Calle Real 4
☎ 922 141512

● **Websites**
Spanish National Tourist
Office:
www.tourspain.es

Local information:
www.cabtfe.es/puntoinfo
www.canary-isles.com
www.ecanarias.com
www.webtenerife.com

NATIONAL HOLIDAYS

J	F	M	A	M	J	J	A	S	O	N	D
2	1	(2)	(1)	2	1	1	1		1	1	3

1 January	Año Nuevo (New Year's Day)
6 January	Los Reyes (Epiphany)
2 February	La Candelaria (Candlemas)
19 March	San José (St Joseph's Day)
March/April	Pascua (Easter) Thu, Fri, Sun of Easter Week, and following Mon
1 May	Dia del Trabajo (Labour Day)
May/June	Corpus Christi
25 July	Santiago (St James' Day)
15 August	Asunción (Assumption)
12 October	Hispanidad (Columbus Day)
1 November	Todos los Santos (All Saints' Day)
6 December	Constitución (Constitution Day)
8 December	Immaculada Concepción (Immaculate Conception)
25 December	Navidad (Christmas)

OPENING HOURS

○ Shops   ● Museums
● Offices   ○ Post Offices
● Banks   ○ Pharmacies

9 AM	10 AM	11 AM	12 PM	1 PM	2 PM	3 PM	4 PM	5 PM	6 PM
9:30	10:30	11:30	12:30	1:30	2:30	3:30	4:30	5:30	

Shops: most shops are open Mon–Sat 9–1, 4–8.
Offices: usually Mon–Fri 9–1, 3–7.
Banks: Mon–Fri 8:30–2, Sat 9–1 (closed Sat 1 Jun–
31 Oct).
Museums: 4–7PM; larger sites open mornings too.
Post Offices: Mon–Fri 8:30–2, Sat 9–1.
Pharmacies: as shops but closed Sat afternoons.
Normally at least one open after hours (rota on door).

**DRIVE ON THE
RIGHT**

**TOILETS
CHARGE**

PUBLIC TRANSPORT

 Buses are always called by their local name, *guaguas* (pronounced wah-wahs). The stops are called *paradas* and are indicated by a letter P. A bus station is called an *estación de guaguas*. Most Tenerife buses are operated by TITSA. Services are fairly frequent and inexpensive on main routes between towns. Off the main roads, and throughout La Gomera, service is intermittent and generally of little use to visitors.

If you plan to use buses a lot, save up to 50 per cent by purchasing a multi-trip TITSA Bono-Bus card.
TITSA hotline (English language) ☎ 922 531300
Main bus stations Avenida Béthencourt, Playa de las Américas ☎ 922 795427
Avenida 3 Mayo 47, Santa Cruz ☎ 922 218122
Calle de Cupido, Puerto de la Cruz ☎ 922 381807
La Laguna ☎ 922 259412
Many of the main attractions operate free shuttle buses to and from the resorts.

 Ferries Transmediterránea (Calle La Marina 59, Santa Cruz ☎ 922 277300): to mainland Spain and other Canary Islands from Santa Cruz; from Los Cristianos to La Gomera.
Estación Jet-Foil (Muelle Norte, Santa Cruz ☎ 922 243012): 80-minute jetfoil to Las Palmas de Gran Canaria.
Estación Hidro-Foil (Los Cristianos harbour ☎ 922 796178): hydrofoils to La Gomera (35 mins).
Ferry Gomera (Los Cristianos harbour ☎ 922 790215): to La Gomera (90 mins).
Fred Olsen (Muelle Ribera, Santa Cruz ☎ 922 628200): to La Gomera and Gran Canaria from Los Christianos and Santa Cruz.

CAR RENTAL

 It is relatively inexpensive to hire a car on Tenerife, but pricier on La Gomera. The small local car firms are efficient (ask for an after-hours emergency number), though the international firms are represented. Drivers must be over 21. A good road map is essential.

TAXIS

 Cabs display a special SP licence plate *(servicio público)*. Some taxi ranks display fares between principal destinations. In addition, taxi drivers offer island tours for up to four passengers; negotiate the fare before you set off.

DRIVING

 Speed limit on motorways:
100–120kph

 Speed limit on other main roads:
100kph

 Speed limit in towns:
40kph

 Seat belts are compulsory for all passengers.
Children under 10 (excluding babies in rear-facing baby seats) must ride in the back seats. If you need child seats, it is strongly advised to book ahead.

 Driving under the influence of alcohol is strictly illegal and random breath tests are carried out; the consequences of being involved in an accident could result in a jail term.

 Unleaded petrol *(sin plomo)* is the norm. Petrol stations on main roads are usually open 24hrs and most take credit cards. Off main roads they may be far apart, closed on Sun, and don't always take credit cards.

 Hired cars and their drivers should all be insured by the hire company. In the event of a breakdown, call the car hire company's emergency number.
Hefty on-the-spot fines are levied for not wearing seat belts, not stopping at a Stop sign or overtaking where forbidden.

PERSONAL SAFETY

Street crime is quite rare in Tenerife and La Gomera but visitors should not be complacent. Uniformed police are always present in tourist areas. The greatest risk is assault or theft by another tourist. Lock doors and windows before going out. Put all valuables in the boot of your car.

- Fire is a risk in hotels – locate the nearest fire exit to your room and ensure it is not blocked or locked.
- Do not leave possessions unattended on the beach or in cars.

Police assistance:
 091 from any call box

TELEPHONES

To call the operator, dial 1009. To use a phone in a bar, simply pay the charge requested at the end of the call – the barman has a meter to check the cost. To use a public pay phone, you'll usually need *una*

 *tarjeta de teléfono*, a phone card – available from tobacconists and similar shops. There are also useful phone offices marked *telefónica internacional* where you pay a clerk after the call.

International Dialling Codes

First dial 00, wait for a change of tone, then dial the country code, for example:

UK	44
Ireland	353
USA	1
Spain	Dial number only

POST

Postboxes are yellow and often have a slot marked *Extranjeros* for mail to foreign countries. Letters and postcards to the UK: 50c (up to 20gms). Air letters and postcards to the US/Canada: 75c (up to 15gms). Letters within Spain: 20c. Buy stamps at tobacconists, souvenir shops or post offices (*correos y telegrafos*).

ELECTRICITY

The voltage is 220–225v.

Sockets take the standard European two-round-pin plugs. Bring an adaptor for any British or American appliances you wish to use with their usual plugs, and Americans should change the voltage setting on appliances, or bring a voltage transformer.

TIPS/GRATUITIES

Yes ✓ No ✗		
Hotels & Restaurants	✗	Incl
Room service	✓	€1–2
Cafe/bar	✓	change
Taxis	✓	10%
Porters	✓	€1–2
Chambermaids	✓	€1–2
Ushers/usherettes at shows & events	✓	change
Hairdressers (women's)	✓	€2–3
Cloakroom/washroom attendant	✓	50c
Tour guide	✓	€2–3

What to Photograph: Pico del Teide is the moody presence in many Tenerife views. The volcanic terrain in Teide National Park provides extraordinary images, as landscapes or close up. Lush colourful vegetation makes a startling backdrop for holiday snaps.
Light: Be aware of the intensity of the light – early morning or evening may produce better effects.
Film: Most popular brands of colour or transparency film of normal speeds are readily available – others may be harder to find. Developing is cheaper in the UK.

HEALTH

Insurance
It is essential to have good medical health cover in case of a medical emergency. Hospital doctors within the state scheme will accept Form E111 from UK residents for free emergency treatment, but the process of reimbursement is complicated and bureaucratic. You may need to give a photocopy of Form E111 to the doctor. To claim on medical insurance you may need to show that you did request treatment under the E111 scheme.

Dental Services
Emergency treatment can be expensive but is covered by most medical insurance (but not by Form E111). Hotel receptionists and holiday reps can generally advise on a local dentist.

Sun Advice
The biggest danger to health here is too much sun. Remember that the Canaries are 700 miles nearer the Equator than southern Spain and on the same latitude as the Sahara. Use generous amounts of sun cream with a high protection factor. A wide-brimmed hat and a T-shirt (even when swimming) are advisable for children.

Medication
Any essential prescribed medications should be taken with you to Tenerife or La Gomera. Well-known over-the-counter proprietary brands of analgesics and popular remedies are available at all pharmacies. All medicines must be paid for, even if prescribed by a doctor.

Safe Water
Tap water is safe all over the islands, except where signs indicate otherwise. The taste may be slightly salty. Bottled water is recommended.

HOSPITALS AND CLINICS

Santa Cruz
Hospital General de Tenerife, Santa Cruz ☎ 922 790401
Hopital Nuestra Señor de Candelaria, Santa Cruz ☎ 922 275563
Puerto de la Cruz and the North
Medical Centre ☎ 900 100090 (free call)
24-hour English-speaking doctors ☎ 900 100090
Playa de las Américas and the South
Centros Medicos del Sur Carretera Gen. del Sur, Playa de las Américas; 24-hour English-speaking doctors ☎ 922 791000

CLOTHING SIZES

Tenerife	UK	Rest of Europe	USA	
46	36	46	36	
48	38	48	38	Suits
50	40	50	40	Suits
52	42	52	42	Suits
54	44	54	44	Suits
56	46	56	46	Suits
41	7	41	8	
42	7.5	42	8.5	Shoes
43	8.5	43	9.5	Shoes
44	9.5	44	10.5	Shoes
45	10.5	45	11.5	Shoes
46	11	46	12	Shoes
37	14.5	37	14.5	
38	15	38	15	Shirts
39/40	15.5	39/40	15.5	Shirts
41	16	41	16	Shirts
42	16.5	42	16.5	Shirts
43	17	43	17	Shirts
34	8	34	6	
36	10	36	8	Dresses
38	12	38	10	Dresses
40	14	40	12	Dresses
42	16	42	14	Dresses
44	18	44	16	Dresses
38	4.5	38	6	
38	5	38	6.5	Shoes
39	5.5	39	7	Shoes
39	6	39	7.5	Shoes
40	6.5	40	8	Shoes
41	7	41	8.5	Shoes

- Always reconfirm your return flight with the airline or holiday rep at least one day before departing.
- Check in at least 90 minutes before flight departure.
- Allow time to return your hire car.

LANGUAGE

People working in the tourist industry, including waiters, generally know some English. In places where few tourists venture, including bars and restaurants in Santa Cruz, it is helpful to know some basic Spanish.

Pronunciation guide: *b* almost like a *v*; *c* before *e* or *i* sounds like *th* otherwise like *k*; *d* can be like English *d* or like a *th*; *g* before *e* or *i* is a guttural *h*, between vowels like *h*, otherwise like *g*; *h* always silent; *j* guttural *h*; *ll* like English *lli* (as in 'million'); *ñ* sounds like *ni* in 'onion'; *qu* sound like *k*; *v* sounds a little like *b*; *z* like English *th*.

hotel	*hotel*	breakfast	*el desayuno*
room	*una habitación*	bathroom	*el cuarto de baño*
single/double/	*individual/doble/*	shower	*la ducha*
twin	*con dos camas*	balcony	*el balcón*
one/two nights	*una noche / dos noches*	reception	*la recepción*
		key	*la llave*
reservation	*una reserva*	room service	*el servicio de habitaciones*
rate	*la tarifa*		

bureau de change	*cambio*	pounds sterling	*libras esterlinas*
post office	*correos*	US dollars	*dólares*
cash machine/ ATM	*cajero automático*	banknote	*un billete de banco*
foreign exchange	*cambio (de divisas)*	traveller's cheques	*cheques de viaje*
foreign currency	*cambio*	credit card	*la tarjeta de crédito*

restaurant	*restaurante*	cheers!	*salud!*
cafe-bar	*bar*	dessert	*el postre*
table	*una mesa*	water	*agua*
menu	*la carta*	(house) wine	*vino (de la casa)*
set main course	*plato combinado*	beer	*cerveza*
		drink	*la bebida*
today's set menu	*el plato del día*	bill	*la cuenta*
wine list	*la carta de vinos*	toilets	*los servicios*

plane	*el avion*	single/return ...	*una ida/de ida y vuelta ...*
airport	*el aeropuerto*		
bus	*el guagua/ autobús*	ticket office	*el despacho de billetes*
ferry	*el ferry*	timetable	*el horario*
terminal	*terminus*	seat	*un asiento*
ticket	*un billete*	reserved seat	*un asiento reservado*

yes	*si*	Is there ...? Do you have ...?	*Hay ...?*
no	*no*		
please	*por favor*	I don't speak Spanish	*No hablo español*
thank you	*gracias*		
Hello/hi	*Hola!*	I am ...	*Soy ...*
Hello/good day	*Buenos dias*	I have ...	*Tengo ...*
Sorry, pardon me	*Perdon*	Help!	*Socorro!*
Bye, see you	*Hasta luego*	How much?	*Cuánto es?*
that's fine	*está bien*	open	*abierto*
What?	*Como?*	closed	*cerrado*

INDEX

Acknowledgements
The Automobile Association would like to thank the following photographers and libraries for their
assistance in the preparation of this book:
MARY EVANS PICTURE LIBRARY 14b; INTERNATIONAL PHOTOBANK 6; PICTURES COLOUR
LIBRARY 90; PIRAMIDES DE GÜIMAR 44; www.euro.ecb.int/ 119 (euro notes).

The remaining photographs are held in the Association's own library (AA PHOTO LIBRARY) and
were taken by:
R MOORE 5b, 7b, 8c, 12c, 15a, 16a, 16b, 17a, 18a, 19, 20a, 20b, 21a, 22a, 23a, 24a, 25a, 25b,
26a, 37b, 38b, 40, 45, 49, 54b, 62b, 68, 72, 75a, 77b, 78b, 79b, 91a, 91b, 92, 93, 94, 95, 96, 97,
98, 99, 100, 101, 102, 103, 104, 105, 106, 107, 108, 109, 110, 111, 112, 113, 114, 115, 116;
C SAWYER 2, 9c, 10b, 12b, 17b, 18b, 21b, 22b, 23b, 26b, 31, 32a, 33a, 33b, 34a, 35a, 35b, 36,
37a, 38a, 39a, 42, 46, 47, 50a, 51a, 51b, 55b, 56a, 56b, 57b, 59b, 59c, 60/61, 63b, 69b, 70b, 70c,
74b, 75b, 80, 81, 82a, 82/83, 83a, 83b, 84, 85a, 85b, 86a, 86b, 87a, 87b, 88, 89a, 89b, 117a, 117b;
J TIMS 1, 5a, 6a, 7a, 8a, 8b, 9a, 9b, 9d, 10a, 11a, 11b, 12a, 13a, 13b, 14a, 15b, 24b, 27a, 27b, 28,
29, 30, 32b, 34b, 34c, 35c, 39b, 41, 43, 48, 50b, 52, 53, 54a, 55a, 57a, 58, 59a, 61, 62a, 63a, 64,
65a, 65b, 66, 67a, 67b, 69a, 70a, 71a, 71b, 71c, 73, 74a, 76, 77a, 78a, 79a, 122a, 122b, 122c.

Dear Essential Traveller

Your comments, opinions and recommendations are very important to us. So please help us to improve our travel guides by taking a few minutes to complete this simple questionnaire.

You do not need a stamp (unless posted outside the UK). If you do not want to cut this page from your guide, then photocopy it or write your answers on a plain sheet of paper.

Send to: **The Editor, AA World Travel Guides, FREEPOST SCE 4598, Basingstoke RG21 4GY.**

Your recommendations...

We always encourage readers' recommendations for restaurants, nightlife or shopping – if your recommendation is used in the next edition of the guide, we will send you a *FREE* **AA** *Essential* **Guide** of your choice. Please state below the establishment name, location and your reasons for recommending it.

_____
_____
_____
_____

Please send me **AA** *Essential* _____
(*see list of titles inside the front cover*)

About this guide...

Which title did you buy?
   AA *Essential* _____
Where did you buy it?_____
When? <u>m m</u> / <u>y y</u>

Why did you choose an AA *Essential* Guide? _____
_____
_____
_____
_____

Did this guide meet your expectations?
   Exceeded ☐   Met all ☐   Met most ☐   Fell below ☐
   Please give your reasons_____
_____
_____
_____

continued on next page...

Were there any aspects of this guide that you particularly liked? ______________

Is there anything we could have done better? ______________

About you...

Name (*Mr/Mrs/Ms*) ______________

Address ______________

______________ Postcode ______________

Daytime tel nos ______________

Which age group are you in?

Under 25 ☐ 25–34 ☐ 35–44 ☐ 45–54 ☐ 55–64 ☐ 65+ ☐

How many trips do you make a year?

Less than one ☐ One ☐ Two ☐ Three or more ☐

Are you an AA member? Yes ☐ No ☐

About your trip...

When did you book? m m / y y When did you travel? m m / y y

How long did you stay? ______________

Was it for business or leisure? ______________

Did you buy any other travel guides for your trip?

If yes, which ones? ______________

Thank you for taking the time to complete this questionnaire. Please send it to us as soon as possible, and remember, you do not need a stamp (*unless posted outside the UK*).

Happy Holidays!

The AA and the Automobile Association Limited, their subsidiaries and any other companies or bodies in which either has an interest ('the AA Group') may use information about you to provide you with details of other products and services, by telephone or in writing. The AA Group as a matter of policy does not release its lists to third parties.

If you do not wish to receive further information please tick the box... ☐

The Atlas

Caroline Jones: the view from the top of Pico del Teide

The Automobile Association
www.theAA.com
The Automobile Association's website offers comprehensive and up-to-the-minute information on insurance, European motoring advice, AA-approved hotels, B&Bs, restaurants and pubs, along with the latest traffic information, detailed UK routes, airport parking, a bookshop and much more.

The Foreign and Commonwealth Office
Country advice, traveller's tips, before you go information, checklists and more.
www.fco.gov.uk

Spanish National Tourist Office
www.tourspain.co.uk
Lots of useful information with an online brochure ordering service.

GENERAL
UK Passport Service
www.ukpa.gov.uk

Health Advice for Travellers
www.doh.gov.uk/traveladvice

UK Travel Insurance Directory
www.uktravelinsurancedirectory.co.uk

BBC – Holiday
www.bbc.co.uk/holiday

The Full Universal Currency Converter
www.xe.com/ucc/full.shtml

Flying with Kids
www.flyingwithkids.com

Links to useful websites
www.discover-tenerife.co.uk

Places to visit, climate, detailed information on the major resorts from accommodation to shopping and taxis.
www.isles.org.uk

How to get there, where to stay and what to see.
www.canaries-live.com

Car hire, golf packages, eating out, excursions, nightlife and shopping.
www.canary-isles.com

All you need to know about the facilities at Los Gigantes marina including diving, dolphin trips and where to eat and shop.
www.losgigantesmarina.com

TRAVEL
Flights and Information
www.cheapflights.co.uk
www.thisistravel.co.uk
www.ba.com
www.worldairportguide.com

English		German
Motorway · Toll junction · Toll station · Junction with number · Motel · Restaurant · Snack bar · Filling station · Parking place with and without WC	Trento	Autobahn · Gebührenpflichtige Anschlussstelle · Gebührenstelle · Anschlussstelle mit Nummer · Rasthaus mit Übernachtung · Raststätte · Erfrischungsstelle · Tankstelle · Parkplatz mit und ohne WC
Motorway under construction and projected with completion date	Date Datum	Autobahn in Bau und geplant mit Datum der Verkehrsübergabe
Dual carriageway (4 lanes)		Zweibahnige Straße (4-spurig)
Trunk road · Road numbers	14 E45	Fernverkehrsstraße · Straßennummern
Important main road		Wichtige Hauptstraße
Main road · Tunnel · Bridge		Hauptstraße · Tunnel · Brücke
Minor roads		Nebenstraßen
Track · Footpath		Fahrweg · Fußweg
Tourist footpath (selection)		Wanderweg (Auswahl)
Shipping route		Schifffahrtslinie

Nature reserve · Prohibited area		Naturschutzgebiet · Sperrgebiet
National park, natural park · Forest		Nationalpark, Naturpark · Wald
Road closed to motor vehicles	X X X X X	Straße für Kfz. gesperrt
Toll road		Straße mit Gebühr
Tourist route · Pass	Weinstraße ⌒1510	Touristenstraße · Pass
Scenic view · Panoramic view · Route with beautiful scenery		Schöner Ausblick · Rundblick · Landschaftlich bes. schöne Strecke

International airport	✈		Internationaler Flughafen
Spa · Swimming pool	♨	⚊	Heilbad · Schwimmbad
Youth hostel · Camping site	△	Å	Jugendherberge · Campingplatz
Golf course · Ski jump	⛳	⚐	Golfplatz · Sprungschanze
Church · Chapel	♁	♁	Kirche im Ort, freistehend · Kapelle
Monastery · Monastery ruin	♦	♦	Kloster · Klosterruine
Palace, castle · Ruin	♦	♦	Schloss, Burg · Schloss-, Burgruine
Tower · Radio-, TV-tower	ⅼ	⍟	Turm · Funk-, Fernsehturm
Lighthouse · Power station	⍭	✦	Leuchtturm · Kraftwerk
Waterfall · Lock	⌁	╪	Wasserfall · Schleuse
Important building · Market place, area	▪	▫	Bauwerk · Marktplatz, Areal
Arch excavation, ruins · Calvary	∴	†	Ausgrabungs- u. Ruinenstätte · Feldkreuz
Dolmen · Menhir · Nuraghe	π	◯ ⚎	Dolmen · Menhir · Nuraghen
Cairn · Military cemetery	☆	⊞	Hünen-, Hügelgrab · Soldatenfriedhof
Hotel, inn, refuge · Cave	⌂	⋂	Hotel, Gasthaus, Berghütte · Höhle

Culture Picturesque town · Elevation	**WIEN** (171)	**Kultur** Malerisches Ortsbild · Ortshöhe
Worth a journey	★★ MILANO	Eine Reise wert
Worth a detour	★ TEMPLIN	Lohnt einen Umweg
Worth seeing	Andermatt	Sehenswert
Landscape Worth a journey	★★ Las Cañadas	**Landschaft** Eine Reise wert
Worth a detour	★ Texel	Lohnt einen Umweg
Worth seeing	Dikti	Sehenswert

```
0          4          8 km
0      2          4 miles
```

Maps © Mairs Geographischer Verlag / Falk Verlag, 73751 Ostfildern

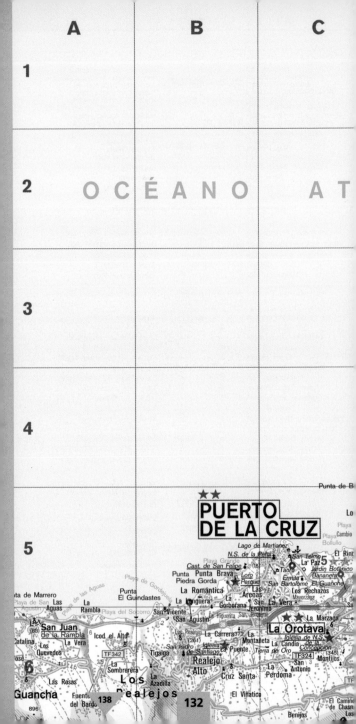

D   **E**   **F**

Roque de Fuera

Roque de Tierra

1

Punta de los Roquetes

Faro de Anaga
Las Palmas   Roque Bermejo
El Draguillo   Casas Blancas
TF134 Benijo   Chamorga
Playa de Benijo

Punta del Drago

Almaciga

Lomo
Chinobre   de las Bodegas
   910   10   Barranco
ailadero   TF 123   de Anosma

Punta de Anaga

d   e   A   n   a   g   a

2

Lomo Bermejo
Semaforo   Punta de Antequera
Iguesté 427   Playa de Antequera
9   563
TF 12   7

El Roquete

Playa de las Gaviotas

Roque   Punta de los Organos
318   ☆ Playa de las Teresitas
San Andrés

3

Dársena Pesquera

★
CRUZ

4

Morro Jable (Fuerteventura) 3½h

Las Palmas de Gran Canaria 1½-4h

5

A T L Á N T I C O

Agaete (Gran Canaria) 1h

6

135

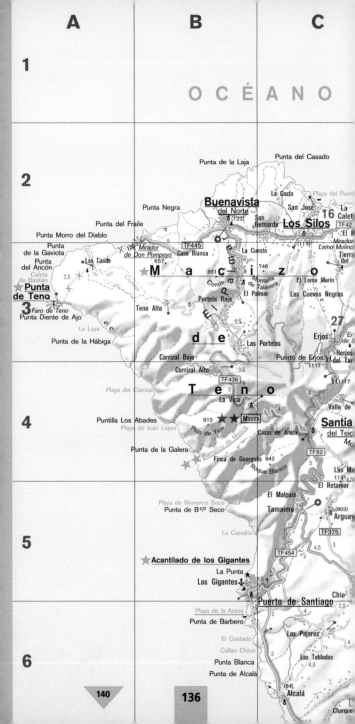

O C É A N O

Punta de la Laja

Punta del Casado

Buenavista del Norte

La Costa

Playa del Puer

San José

Los Silos

La Calet

TF 42

16

Punta Negra

San Bernardo

El

Punta del Fraile

Lomo Molino

Tierra del

Punta Morro del Diablo

Mirador de Don Pompeyo

TF445

La Cuesta

Punta de la Gaviota

657

Casa Blanca

746

Punta del Ancón

Las Casas

851

M a c i z o

El Lomo Morin

Caleta de Bastián

2,5

Conde

Montaña de Talavera

Las Cuevas Negras

★ **Punta de Teno**

Portela Baja

El Palmar

Faro de Teno

Teno Alto

El

27

Punta Diente de Ajo

Erjos

Er de

La Laya

Pa

2,5

Herjos del Tar

Punta de la Hábiga

d e

Las Portelas

Puerto de Erjos

1117

Carrizal Bajo

(1117)

Carrizal Alto

3,5

TF436

Playa del Carrizal

T e ñ o

3

Valle de

La Vica

Puntilla Los Abades

915

★★ Masca

Santia

Playa de Juan López

Pico de Yejn

del Teic

Mo

Punta de la Galera

Casas de Araza

TF82

Finca de Guergués 942

5

Roque Blanco

Las M

1131

El Retamar

El Malpaís

Playa de Berranco Seco

Tamaimo

(903)

Argua

Punta de Bº Seco

La Canalita

TF375

4,5

TF454

★ **Acantilado de los Gigantes**

La Punta

Chío

2,5

Los Gigantes ⚓

Puerto de Santiago

Playa de la Arena

2

4

Punta de Barbero

Los Pajares

4

El Costado

Callao Chico

3

Las Tabladas

4,5

Punta Blanca

Punta de Alcalá

(84)

Alcalá

Charque

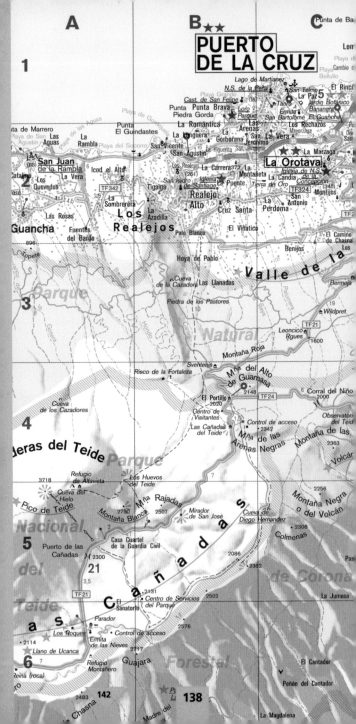

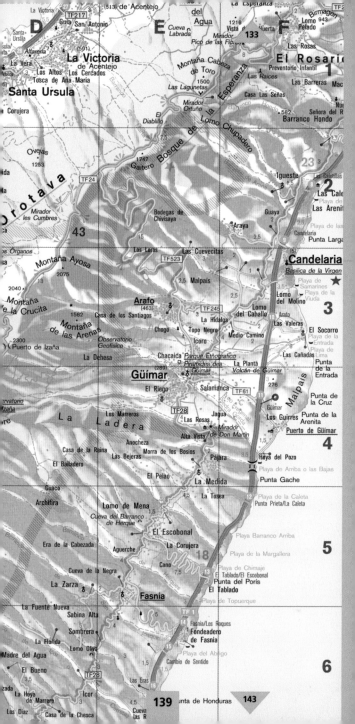

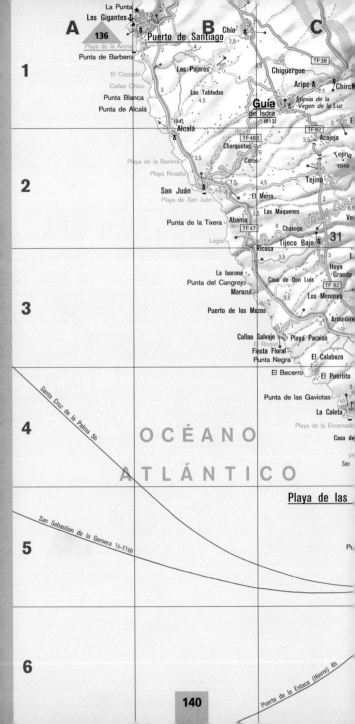

A

La Punta
Los Gigantes
136
Playa de la Arena
Punta de Barbero

El Costado
Callao Chico
Punta Blanca
Punta de Alcalá

(84)
Alcalá

Playa de la Barrera
Playa Rosalía

San Juán
Playa de San Juán

Punta de la Tixera **Abama**
TF47
Lagial

B

1,5
Puerto de Santiago
Chío
2,5

2
4
1,5

Los Pajares
4
Las Tabladas
4,5

3
Guía
de Isora
(612)

TF468
Charquetas
9
Corco
3,5

1,5
4,5

El Morro
3,5
Los Máquenes
6 **Chasogo**
Tijoco Bajo
Ricasa
3,5

La Isorana
Punta del Cangrejo
Marazul

Puerto de los Mozos

Callao Salvaje
El Roque
Fiesta Floral
Punta Negra

El Becerro

Punta de las Gaviotas

La Caleta
Playa de la Enramada

C

1

TF38
Chiguergue
Aripe
2,5
Church
Iglesia de la
Virgen de la Luz

2
TF82
3,5
Acojeja

Tejina
1049

Tejina
3

3
Ve

31

L
**Hoya
Grande**
TF 82
Casa de Don Luis
Los Menores
3,5
3

Armeñin
3

Playa Paraíso
El Calabozo

El Puertito
3

Casa de

San

Playa de las

Pu

Santa Cruz de la Palma 5h

O C É A N O

A T L Á N T I C O

San Sebastián de la Gomera ½-1½h

Puerto de la Estaca (Hierro) 4h

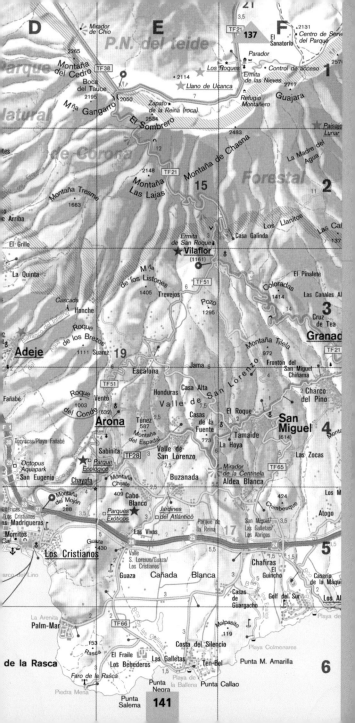

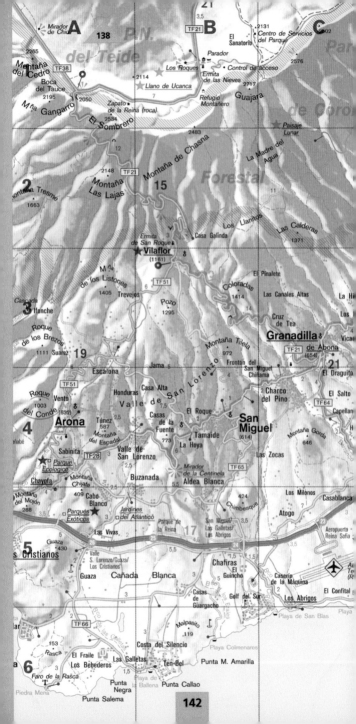

A
Mirador de Chío
138
P.N.
del Teide
2265
Montaña del Cedro
TF38
Boca del Tauce
2195
2050
Mña Gangarro
El Sombrero
2584

B
2131
TF21
3,5
El Sanatorio
Centro de Servicios del Parque
602
Parador
Los Roques
Ermita de las Nieves
2114
Llano de Ucanca
7
Zapato de la Reina (roca)
Refugio Montañero
2717
Guajara
2576

C
Par
Control de acceso
Paisaje Lunar
de Coron

2483
La Madre del Agua

2
Montaña Tresme
1663
2148
TF21
Montaña Las Lajas
15
Montaña de Chasna
Forestal
11
Los Llanitos
Casa Galinda
Las Calderas
1371

Ermita de San Roque
★ Vilaflor
(1161)
Mña de los Listones
1405
Trevejos
TF51
6
El Pinalete
Coloradas
1414
Las Canales Altas
La Hi
Los

3
Cascada
Ifonche
Roque de los Brezos
1111 Suarez
19
6
Escalona
Pozo
1295
14
Cruz de Tea
Montaña Tilela
972
Frontón del
San Miguel
Chiñama
Granadilla
de Abona
(654)
21
Vica
El Draguito

Jama
5
Valle de San Lorenzo

4
Roque del Conde
1003
TF51
Vento
(632)
Arona
Túnez
587
Montaña del Espadal
Sabinita
TF28
Chayofa
Montaña Chijafe
Honduras
Casa Alta
Casas de la Fuente
Valle de San Lorenzo
2,5
Buzanada
5,5
Casa Alta
El Roque
2
Tamaide
(614)
773
La Hoya
6
Mirador de la Centinela
TF65
Aldea Blanca
San Miguel
(614)
4
1
Charco del Pino
El Salto
Capellan
TF64
Montaña Gorda
646
Las Zocas
H

5
Montaña del Mojón
288
3,5
409 Cabo Blanco
Parqués Exóticos
3
Jardines del Atlántico
Las Vivas
Parque de la Reina
17
2,5
Chimbesqua
424
Los Milonos
Atogo
7
Casablanca
3
Aeropuerto Reina Sofía
s Cristianos
Guaza
430
Valle
S. Lorenzo/Guaza/
Los Cristianos
Guaza
2
5,5
25
Cañada
Blanca
3
5,5
24
San Miguel/
Las Galletas/
Los Abrigos
3,5
3,5
1,5
1,5
Chafiras
El Guincho
5
Golf del Sur
3
Caserío de la Máquina
2
Los Abrigos
Ae
Te
(R)
El Confital
Playa

6
153
Rasca
Faro de la Rasca
Piedra Mena
TF66
El Fraile
Los Bebederos
Las Galletas
1,5
Punta Negra
Punta Salema
Casas de Guargacho
Malpasito
119
Costa del Silencio
Ten-Bel
Playa de la Ballena
Punta Callao
Playa Colmenares
Punta M. Amarilla
Playa de San Blas

142